He Rules the Nations
A BOOK OF PROPHACY

Book 1

Psalm 22:27-28. All the ends of the world shall remember and turn to the Lord, and all the families of the nations shall worship before You. For the kingdom is the Lord's. And He rules over the nations. Nkjv.

ANTHONY WHARTON

Copyright © 2019 by Anthony Wharton.

ISBN Softcover   978-1-949723-90-8

All rights reserved. No part of this book may be reproduced or transmitted in any form or by any means, electronic or mechanical, including photocopying, recording, or by any information storage and retrieval system without express written permission from the author, except in the case of brief quotations embodied in critical reviews and certain other non-commercial uses permitted by copyright law.

Printed in the United States of America.

To order additional copies of this book, contact:
Bookwhip
1-855-339-3589
https://www.bookwhip.com

CONTENTS

A. Introduction iv

B. Words of Prophesy 1

C. Prayer of Salvation 124

D. Direction for new members of the family 125

E. The first year with Jesus 125

F. Prayer for your nation 125

G. Prayer for the Church. 126

H. THE FRAY. A report on witchcraft 129

I. Anthony Wharton Contacts 147

Introduction

God and His Son Jesus the Christ still rule the earth. He is the true King above all earthly kings and He lords over every move on the earth that is done in secret or in the open. Nothing escapes Him because Jesus the Christ has the true all seeing eyes. He is the only true illuminated and enlightened One so all others are false and deceived by the father of lies. Powerful nations have come and gone but Jesus still rules and orchestrates.

Where is Babylon, where is Egypt, where are the Persians, where are Alexander and his Greeks, where is Rome and where are those who claim to be rulers and conquers on the earth. They are all gone but God is still alive and He rules and orchestrates as He chooses.

The plans and strategies of man will come to nothing without the approval of the Creator of man and all the earth. You who are baptized into wicked and dark things know that He sees you and

He knows you. He is still the God of judgment and wrath because of wickedness and evil on the earth due to sin. But He is also the God of pure and unconditional love. His love forgives the greatest personal and national sins; His love covers a multitude of sins and the sins of multitudes. You who work in dark places and do dark things know that the eyes of Jesus sees you. You believe you have a brotherhood or a sisterhood but when Jesus sets you free from the deception of satan you will experience true enlightenment. Know that satan has a counterfeit for the true things of Jesus. You have been deceived but true and pure enlightenment that comes through Jesus alone is available to you. All nations will be judged but there is an escape when we come to true repentance and the acknowledgement that Jesus Christ is Lord and ruler of the earth.

Your government cannot outthink Him, your military is nothing before Him and all your wealth already belongs to Him so Jesus cannot be bought or sold. Nations have been judged and nations will be judged but there is still time for repentance. The false god of the dollar will fail you, the false gods of wood and stone cannot save you and God and His Son created the sun, moon, stars and all other things so why worship the created things when the Creator is greater.

Religion has deceived millions and generations. Even the good things of religion does not impress All Mighty God because He knows the true motive and hidden intent.

There are nations marked for goodness and blessings because He is the living God that can pour out blessings.

Jesus rules in the affairs of men.

Anthony Wharton.

Daniel 4:17 ... In order that the living may know that the Most High rules in the kingdom of men ... Nkjv.

Words of Prophesy

Wednesday 10th April 2002.
Trinidad and Tobago. "The systems that man has set up will fail before his eyes. Face to face. There is a reformation coming to this land but first things will get worse. There is going to be a shaking of the systems by the root, the foundations will be shaken. Things will get worse before man turns to the One whose name is on this land. There is a shaking, shaking, shaking. Man's systems will be shaken to the foundation. Reformation is coming, Reformation is coming but their has to be a breaking down first. God wants His people to stay faithful in the midst of everything. His will, will be established. A government in His honor but their has to be a shaking first."

Thursday 6th June 2002.
God showed me civil war in Ethiopia but it is really the attack of the enemy on the Church. I prayed that the demons behind it be rebuked and their work destroyed.

* * * * * * *

God showed me Tanzania and He said: "He would put people in key positions to bring reform. Tanzania in turmoil, Tanzania in turmoil but I will reform. The people cry out and I have heard their cry. My Church, My Church, I have heard My Church."

Sunday 9th June 2002.
"I will reform the nation of Tanzania and use it mightily."

Friday 21st June 2002.
"The judgment of God is coming to Trinidad and Tobago."

Sunday 30th June 2002.
"The nations will be one. One day the West Indies will be one. The power of God and unity. It will be done."

Friday 12th July 2002.
"I am going to judge England says the Lord."

Sunday 15th September 2002.
The Holy Spirit spoke through Apostle Dr Turnel Nelson.
"They wont believe you will write a book."

Wednesday 16th April 2003.
"Trinidad and Tobago you are going through birth pains. Before the birth of a brand new nation, birth pains. The nation will be reformed but the woman must go through birth pains. Trials upon trials, trials and tribulations. First the pains must get worse for the Church and for the nation."

Sunday 16th January 2005.
"You will roll along in Me. I will do a work in you and exalt you. It will be quick. Mighty exploits shall you do. I place a shield in front of you, behind you and at your sides. A strong man. You love to preach but you will do more than that. The last shall be first."

Sunday 19th June 2005.
I saw a mountain crumbling and falling into the sea and under the mountain was another mountain that looked like crystal. The crystal mountain then crumbled and fell apart so what was hidden in the crystal mountain was exposed and it was the Church.

Then God said "I am going to expose My Church with great power and might I then saw the sea drawing back and peoples and nations were exposed. The sea kept drawing back and great multitudes of peoples were seen that was under the sea. The Church was high above the people and out of it came great light. The light kept going out towards the people and exposing darkness.

Then there was a great rush towards the Church. Many made it in but not all.

Matthew 5:14. You are the light of the world. A city that is set on a hill cannot be hidden. Nkjv.

Micah 4:1-2. Now it shall come to pass in the latter days that the mountain of the Lord's house shall be established on the top of the mountains, and shall be exalted above the hills; and peoples shall flow to it. Many nations shall come and say, Come and let us go up to the mountain of the Lord, To the house of the God of Jacob; He will teach us His ways, And we shall walk in His paths. For out of Zion the law shall go fourth, and the word of the Lord from Jerusalem. Nkjv.

<u>Sunday 28th January 2007.</u>
… and landed in South America and their was an explosion and all of South America was ablaze and the fire was consuming. I saw false churches falling down, especially the roman empire that masquerades as true Christianity.

The Holy Spirit then said to me "it is coming down, it is coming down."

<u>Friday 23rd March 2007.</u>
This morning I saw the island of Barbados being baptized. The whole island was submerged under sea water and brought back up again.

"I will take them deep in My Spirit and bring them up again. Changes, changes, changes even systems will be changed."

<u>Saturday 5th May 2007.</u>
I saw the Island of St Lucia being flipped over and over in the sea. God said "I am turning things around."

<u>Sunday 26th August 2007.</u>
"You who speak Spanish, soon there will be a flood and you will speak My language says the Lord."

* * * * * *

"Land of the rising sun I shall break your sickle. China, in a time and in a season I will make your burden light." I looked into China and I saw many roads leading out four ways.

* * * * * *

"The man with the German tongue. The wall was removed but the spirit of the wall is still in your mind. I will do a work says the Lord, true freedom."

* * * * * * *

"Turkey, your mountains will tremble and your wealth will be exposed."

* * * * * *

"Be anxious no more Mexican man for I am going to visit your sons and they will walk the earth and be respected. Do not look to the north, I am greater."

* * * * * * *

"Belgium, I am going to move you out of place so you can seek my face. I saw Belgium shake and move. They cried out but the cry was upward towards God."

* * * * * *

"Trinidad, you carry My name but I will not tolerate the shame. Repent."

* * * * * *

"Islands of the English I am going to shake you. You once had supremacy but it is gone. I am going to shake you. You have allowed darkness to come in and stifle My voice. How dare you. I am going to shake you. I want to do a work. I want to restore the glory."

* * * * * * *

"Unless America repents their worst fear will overtake them and subdue them and they will cry out to other nations for help. Do not test Me says the Lord. You say you trust in God. Do not mock Me. Do not be deceived."

I saw the American flag flying high in the atmosphere above the earth. Then it caught on fire and the stars of the flag fell to the ground and eagles came and took the stars and scattered them all over the world.

* * * * * * *

"Brazil, Brazil I have seen your lewdness and misconduct. Repent or the jungle will overtake you. The things you cannot see will come out of the jungle and overtake you."

I looked into Brazil and I saw naked spirits running around and then other spirits came and held on to them and took them into the jungle and they were never seen again.

* * * * * * *

"You were prisoners down under and the colony became a nation. I want to use you because from down under you can hold up great things. I want to make your voice powerful because I want to use you to speak for me. Look where I took you from. I can do greater."

In a vision I saw Australia lift out of the sea, circle the earth and sat back in place again.

* * * * * * *

I see Pakistan divided in half with a line drawn in the middle of the land. Both sides are angry and they rush towards each other for war. It looked like civil war and India will have military build up on the border to protect itself.

****

I saw a great sward come down in Iran and then their was a great explosion. Women crying, the men are on fire and I smell the burning flesh. The wind will carry the scent and the surrounding nations will tremble.

"Never again will you despise Me. Never again, never again. A generation is lost."

****

"I speak to the earth,
I speak to the nations,
I created you,
You are still mine,
Do not be deceived."

Tuesday 28th August 2007.
"To the far east I will draw back the waters and release the flesh eaters and they will devour the people. But many will turn to Me because I will also send healing. I will judge one and heal the other. When one is dead two shall be saved. They have not turned from the little man with no life."

****

"I will cut off the head of the madman. Venezuela, I will plow your land and cause you to see Me in a new way.

I see bombs and missiles falling on Venezuela.

"Run to the hills, run to the hills. I am not against you says the Lord but I am plowing your ground."

I saw a great ball come out of the sky and hit the land and it caused a great crater in the earth. In time beautiful flowers grew and came out of it.

* * * * * * *

America, I see a pestilence rising in the heartland and it will devour much and spread even to the cities. "It shall not be stopped."

* * * * * * *

"Hawaii, the time is coming again. volcano, volcano. Out of the sea great fire."

I see fire on the waters, dead fishes all around.

* * * * * * *

"Jakarta, there is wealth in the soil. I will expose it, I will expose your wealth."

Sunday 2nd September 2007.
I see a little flame in Spain.

"A little Church will produce a great flame that will change their language."

* * * * * * *

"The web, the spider, the spider. I am removing the web from over France and their will be great rejoicing and a burst of missions with great signs and wonders. O French man the Lord is about to visit and He will fill you up and send you out like arrows that will not miss the target."

* * * * * * *

"Belgium, hold still, hold still because after the shaking a great blossoming. My radiance will shine on you and keep you."

* * * * * * *

"Germany, I am extending your borders. An out pouring and rolling over."

I see the fire of God pouring out of Germany into surrounding nations and demons fleeing, especially government.

Thursday 13th September 2007.
"Like an arrow I am sending St Kitts forward, like an arrow. I am straightening them out and they will be launched like an arrow."

* * * * * * *

"Guadeloupe, I will give the sea your land so you will know I rule."

* * * * * * *

"Martinique, the tourist will stop and your economy will drop but it is for a time. I will restore glory."

* * * * * * *

"Tobago, I will send a storm to shake you again but I will warn you before hand so you can repent. I see all says the Lord, I see what the House of Assembly is doing."

Saturday 15th September 2007.
"St Kitts & Nevis, for a season I will break your arm and you will not get help from the outside."

* * * * * * *

"Jamaica, you have intoxicated the world but I am going to do some rooting up, make some changes. I am going to humble you. You will feel My whip but the child must be humbled."

Sunday 16th September 2007.
"St Vincent, like a volcano I will shake you so the hands from the outside that control you will be removed."

* * * * * * *

"France, I am going to make your military stronger and use you to help other nations maintain peace."

* * * * * * *

"Geneva, Geneva, you lied and I am going to expose it."

* * * * * * *

Tuesday 18th September 2007.
"France, I am changing the guard."

* * * * * * *

"Great Britain, I have striped you of your "great" so you will be dependent on Me again."

Thursday 27th September 2007.
"Jamaica, I am going to break your pride. I am going to break your donkey I am going to break your song."

* * * * * * *

"Israel, you have forgotten Me but I have not forgotten you. I will chasten you, and chasten you, and chasten you. I have not forgotten you. I am coming to put My order in place."

* * * * * * *

"O great wall, you were built to keep your enemies out but you locked yourself in and even today you till try to be locked away from the rest of the world. Your mysteries will no longer be mysteries and your secrets will be known because your spiritual wall is bigger and higher than the great wall but I remove the foundation stones so the inner structure can fall. The great wall will crumble, the spiritual wall will crumble."

* * * * * * *

"America, you were once separated states but came together in strength. I will scatter you says the Lord, repent!"

Thursday 18th October 2007.
I saw a white cloth stretched out and fanning the earth from up in space. God said:

"I am stirring up the atmosphere. Storms and hurricanes are coming. Get ready, get ready says the Lord. I will blow on nations in a physical way to throw down wickedness. What nation is stronger than Me, what nation is mightier than My breath. As a storm that touches everything I will blow across the lands and root up. I speak it and I bring it to pass soon."

Wednesday 12th December 2007.
"I am going to shake Trinidad says the Lord. The mountains shall shake, buildings shall fall. Lives will be lost and lives will be saved but I will shake Trinidad. I am a just God and I have no favorites."

Saturday 19th January 2008.
"I write many books say's the Lord and I give to the Churches in Trinidad and Tobago. Many books will come out of the Churches and travel the globe. Many nations will look to this nation. The nation with the answers."

Friday 18th April 2008.
"An increase of pestilence is coming on the earth for the sins of many have angered Me but I will hold in My hands the righteous and they will flourish so fear not and see Me do the works I have promised."

Sunday 27th April 2008.
"A multitude of prophets will rise out of Australia because of the worship."

Wednesday 14th May 2008.
"This land that is named after Me will receive another aspect of My glory. I will cause the government to change."

Thursday 12th June 2008.
I looked into Germany and I saw men in military uniform with red arm bands marching down a main road. Then I heard: "We are planning a comeback Nazi politics is planning a comeback. We are here to stay and we shall not be moved. This is our mother land."

Friday 18th July 2008.
I saw a horse, a cow and a camel walking together. God said "These are the strength of three nations." The horse was a dark glistening stallion that was wild and untamable. The cow was white, overly fat and slow but its head was towards the ground as if it was carrying shame and ridicule. The camel pranced around in pride with a smile on his face.
The three formed a league that the other nations did not know about and they traded and sustained each other. Their money was equal and they enjoyed each others company until an angry rhino came and trample on their league and it was destroyed.
The cow fell on its left side and died. The horse got a broken left leg and limped away never to be seen again and the camel rode away in the desert with much anger.
The rhino then stands in the place the others once stood in and he lifted up his horn. Then he died and become dust. The place they

all once held became desolate as the desert sands and nothing ever grows or prospered their.

This is about three nations and the mighty strength of one nation that is to come with power. A nation that already exists but its anger is brewing.

Wednesday 20th August 2008.
I had a vision of Borneo and I saw the spirits of Islam and Hinduism coming together and dancing with each other.

"They are forming an alliance to come against Christianity, says the Lord. Many evil plans are plotted even in the hospitals they are plotting wickedness to Christians when they come in for treatment. But My Spirit will rise and crush the plans and cut the ribbons that form the alliance. Borneo will breathe, Borneo will breathe and My truth will be established."

I also saw the earth open and fire came out and devour people then it stopped but then it happened again.

"Because of My grace I stopped what was meant to destroy but they have not repented so many will burn. I stopped it in the past but not again."

* * * * * * *

"Beijing. I am using it says the Lord many are being ministered to. Many reaching out with My gospel. I am their among them, many will know Me, many will return to their nation with My Spirit."

Saturday 4th October 2008.
I was standing in a high place above the earth: "Germany is about to be expanded, Germany is about to be expanded."

* * * * * * *

I saw in the atmosphere above China an anti clockwise spinning. Then God said: "I am taking them back to the drawing board to root up, to restore. I will cause them to visit old things so future history will change for My plans for China is great. The worship of man will face the sword and idols shall crumble says the Lord. For a time and another time I shall leave them hungry until they hunger for Me and My words which is life and a preserver of life. The ships of trade shall depart and their airport shall become empty."

I see a man looking out to sea looking for ships to come but none is coming. "For I have destined it says the Lord for soon famine and soon life. I turn the page for a restructuring and a rewriting of the land. O how they will know that I am good and My workings are for generations."

Tuesday 7th October 2008.
"Argentina has fallen,
Argentina has fallen,
The prince of Argentina has fallen,
I cut the mountains,
I weaken their strength,
It is fallen, it is fallen,
The prince is fallen."

Wednesday 15th October 2008.
"Uganda, I remove the ties that bind you and I give your hands free access to what is stored up for you. Your past is beneath you. Much awaits you for I see and hear your heart beat and I will expose the lies of those who control your money.

Uganda, your mothers had to carry heavy burdens. Many watched their children die but all is not lost for I will restore ten times the amount. Your population will explode and with this will come much power where you can give help to other nations. From the heart will come much access to other nations and I will use you as an example to them."

* * * * * * *

"For you have seen that My word is true and never empty says the Lord. For I have disciplined you America but must I continue? You have cared for things that oppose Me and your gods have no respect for Me. For your waters will run red for your stubbornness and the hands of your military will become weak so another man will lead you to the well your forefathers have left behind. I take no pleasure in your children paying the price but you have continually dishonored Me. How can you be honored when you have dishonored Me? You removed My name by removing My word. I established you generations ago but you have stopped a generation from knowing Me. Other nations will stop and wonder, but it is Me. Freedom of speech doesn't mean freedom to stop Me. I AM GOD."

* * * * * * *

"France, I have seen what you have done underground and the things you have buried for future purposes. The land can become waste with pollutants and the land that was meant to sustain you will not yield. The earth is a blessing to bear much fruit but a man made plague can curse the land. You can see a greater day if you save the land. For I want to bless you with much yield. I want to over run the mountains with pure waters. Can't you see what's happening I want to return My hand to the land.
I will expose your catacombs for all to see. On the surface you look beautiful and holy but much history you hide. For the Roman order will be brought to disorder says the Lord."

Wednesday 29th October 2008.
"Trinidad and Tobago. I will cut this land in half and a valley will be formed. Out of the valley new things."

I see a valley between two mountain peaks and in the valley fresh flowers tall and strong with the colors of white, green, yellow, blue and red. Around the valley lush green grass.

"But I will shake the land from the sea to the mountain. The temple will be shaken, the mosque will be shaken and the false church will be shaken."

Tuesday 4th November 2008.
"I am about to do a work in Trinidad & Tobago says the Lord where I am going to make the Churches one. Where I am going to rise up a standard and one movement. For I have waited long says the Lord but now they are ready. So I am going to graft each one to the other and they, My house, shall walk as one under Me by My Spirit says the Most High."

Sunday 9th November 2008.
"I will give Barack Obama two terms says the Lord and he is the man to bring many changes not only in America but a great example on the earth. He is a marker for Me that a new breed of people will rise to leadership and be strong in love for My purpose on the earth. No harm will come to him for I am with him and his family. Their will be traitors in his camp but they will fail and be exposed for I see all things and My hand of protection is with him, My chosen."

Tuesday 11th November 2008.
"For the waves are about to come in on Suriname says the Lord. The waves of My glory are about to go over the land. The fire of My revival will bloom and spread in that nation. From the sea wave after wave of My glory will sweep across the land says the Lord."

* * * * * * *

"I am spreading My goodness upon Jamaica. They will receive the favor of international help says God and much blessings are going to pour into the land of Jamaica. For the Church have risen up and taken their place, so now the land will be blessed and I am stemming the violence to go no further, for I send My cloud to saturate the land and do what the politicians could not do for they will know that God is in the land and I have taken over with My love and might for the internal war is over. I am visiting the gangs and those who supply the arms and ammunitions and much crocked police officers will be exposed for they have caused much untimely deaths and sorrow to those who are innocent. I am removing the hiding places and all covers will be no more."

* * * * * * *

"I will shake the foundation in Russia and I will cause the Church to have a voice like never before. I will cause them to listen to My voice in Russia says the Lord."

* * * * * * *

"I prophesy to you Yemen, that I will raise up a woman among you to speak for Me on the radio and in the newspapers. She will not be stopped."

Thursday 13th November 2008.
I was thinking about America and the Lord said: "They have removed My name says the Lord so I have removed My grace. Greater things are coming against them. Ten years of extreme weather changes where lives will be lost like never before."

Saturday 15th November 2008.
I see a torpedo traveling under sea with the words CSSR on it. The torpedo is traveling towards a black looking rock but there is a light shining in the distance. The torpedo hits the rock and destroys it but the torpedo does not explode and continues to travel towards the light in the distance. It looks as if the light sucks in the torpedo and turns it around and it starts traveling in the direction it came from then

explodes underwater. This creates a mushroom affect on the surface of the water which changes the weather and creates tidal waves.

Wednesday 26th November 2008.
"The lies of scientific research will be exposed and they will acknowledge Me. They will come to the conclusion that it took a Great and Supreme God to create all that is seen on the earth. Science will acknowledge that I am Creator and what was believed in the past is a lie."

Friday 19th December 2008.
"Brazil, I cut the top off of your mountain and I cause your volcano to erupt and spill over. A pouring over and a pouring out says the Lord. I am about to pour out of you much goodness from the things that are great treasures in you for I will cut off the top of the high places and much of your wealth will be exposed."

Tuesday 23rd December 2008.
I saw skeletons in Nazi Gestapo uniforms marching in Germany and saying: "We are coming back, we are coming back. Authority has been given to us we are coming back." I also saw them marching with mantles being held upside down. They also said: "death, death we bring death."

Thursday 1st January 2009.
"My house, My house will come to desolation. Warn them of My coming wrath for man have lifted up themselves as gods directing and misdirecting the lives of others. Many speak on My behalf but I gave them no word to speak so their own words I have sifted and found no good thing says the Lord.
When will they know and when will they understand that I direct and I fulfill promises."

Wednesday 7th January 2009.

"I call the nations to repentance says God for many of them refuse to bow to Me. I have piped and blown the flute and they have not listened. I have blown the horn O so loudly and they put their hands over their ears. I call the nations to My presence and their children and they turned away and answer another invitation.

I stretched out My hands towards them but they laughed because what they have seems to be greater. So I clench My fist and the favor now becomes a war. A war here and a war over their, a battle here and a battle else where.

I clench My fist, for many nations will receive no more favor. The season is upon them and the time is now.

I have called and called and I have knocked on many doors but they refuse to answer so how can they receive, O the blind ones how can they receive.

I shaked a few to get their attention but their attention was on the agendas that had no solution."

I see swords in the atmosphere above nations and on every sword have the date and time to execute the will of God.

* * * * * * *

"Many nations have wrestled with Me and lost. Many nations shouted at Me when I spoke to them and many turned their backs and walked away into darkness with anger.

Throw the line and pull them in, throw the line and pull them out. For a season is coming where My fire will come from the sky and nothing will stop it."

I see nations sealed so no destruction will come then I see nations marked for the sword to come down upon.

Friday 9th January 2009.
"Russia is about to be shaken. Many earthquakes, the land is about to be shaken says the Lord. For they will know when they reject Me they reject life. A shaking, a shaking, a shaking, great catastrophe. Mineral wealth will be swallowed up and oil wells will fall. The wealth of the land will be shaken soon, son, soon.
I crack a nuclear reactor and I cause a spill just as My blood was spilt. For the affects of the shaking will be felt for many years and they will turn to Me. The land to the north."

Saturday 17th January 2009.
"I am going to expose great corruption in the Japanese government says the Lord. I will soon, soon expose corruption in the government of Japan."

* * * * * * *

"I change the culture of the fathers. I pave a new road for the Church in Australia. I give new insight for them to look into. I cause them to have greater influence, I change many things. A stronger Church is about to be born, a stronger Church."

* * * * * * *

"Many works being done in Madagascar grieve Me says the Lord so I strike My fist on the land. They have stained the land and they have hissed at Me like a snake. They have tried to tame Me and many sit in My place but I am God. Many floods are coming on the land and I will wash man and beast. I cleanse the land says the Lord."

* * * * * * *

"The Shaman has done his work for many years but now it is time for My work. O ancient name I have not forgotten you, I will break the arrow and I take away the spear. Humbly I call you Ethiopia, humbly I call you for we were once friends but you looked the other way you turned the other way. Will you look to Me again, will you look into My eyes again O ancient name. I call you again and again I call."

* * * * * * *

Tanzania, I see hands parting the dark clouds above you and a great light is shining through. It is not the sun, it looks like the sun but it is a greater light. The light comes closer and closer to your land and dark things like snakes and devils run out. Many run into the sea and cause disruptions and many are pierced through with arrows that look like light and they die in the land.

"A day is gone and another day comes Tanzania for I rid your land and I cleanse your people. For I bring My warmth and the harshness is removed."

I see a man with darkness coming off of him as someone takes off a shirt and a new shirt, white comes on him and he runs off rejoicing speaking in his native language.

* * * * * * *

"Morocco, I have given you prestige. I have given you style but yet many hidden things you hide from the rest of the world. For I close one door to the north and I open many other doors for I still favor you Morocco."

Tuesday 10th February 2009.
I see two great hands lift Japan out of the sea and shake it. "Now that I have disrupted their peace says God now they will look to Me. I want to restructure their structure, I want to shape and mold but they are a stubborn people says God, they are a stubborn people."

* * * * * * *

In Hawaii I see deep beneath the island a worm (demon) coming up from deep beneath the earth and this worm is releasing poison from its mouth and the poison is killing the pineapple crops by poisoning the roots.

"For I do not send this thing for the enemy has launched an attack. Who has eyes to see let them see says the Lord. Pray for the Church and alert the Church for the Church in that land has the power to stop it says the Lord."

* * * * * * *

I see Jerusalem as a cake and two hands took it up and broke the cake in two equal pieces. The piece in the left hand was being eaten and the piece in the right hand was placed back on the earth.

"Two equal pieces I call you but only one has favor and flavor with Me says the Lord. One is pleasing to Me and one is not. Two are equal but only one pleasing."

* * * * * * *

Madagascar, I see a fist pounding the land. "Give up; give up your rebellion says the Lord. You hiss at Me and snap at Me. Give up your rebellion. Madagascar give up your rebellion."

I see Madagascar locked in a bottle and two great hands are shaking the bottle and there are also dirt in the bottle. The bottle is opened and Madagascar is poured out with woe, wailing and torment.

Monday 16th February 2009.
I see the nation of Israel lift out of its geographical place and rise in the atmosphere. The whole nation travels over nations of the earth and water like crystal is falling from Israel on the nations. It is as if Israel is raining on the nations as it goes over them. Then it returns to its geographical area and sits in its original place.

Then a burst of light with rays come out of Israel and the nations that it rained on also burst out with light. I hear the word "glory". I see people in darkness and with darkness on them. The darkness leaves them and there is dancing and rejoicing.

"I give Israel the authority to water many nations. They will even help their enemies."

* * * * * * *

I see a finger from heaven spinning Egypt anti clockwise. "I am taking them back to fix the things that should have been fixed. Egypt will be strong again. Egypt will be strong again."

* * * * * * *

Tanzania, I see belts like the ones around a mans waist being pulled from the land and there is great rejoicing.

* * * * * * *

"Mozambique, cast out your nets into the sea for greater things you are about to catch. I am going to reform you Mozambique and lift you up higher."

I see a great net is cast out into the ocean and it lay's their for a time. Then the net grabs like the hand of a man and pulls. All sorts of riches are brought from the ocean to the surface of the land.

* * * * * * *

I see under the surface of Japan they are driving construction piles into the ground to make the land sturdy. I see a huge hand grab the piles from under the surface of the earth and brake them. Then Japan cracks in half from the east to the west.

* * * * * * *

"More is coming at another day. Turn the page and write My witness to the earth. Write My witness to the earth says the Lord."

Thursday 26th February 2009.
I saw a man using a shovel to take coals out of a furnace and the coals symbolized Pakistan. He was throwing the coals on the ground to cool off.

* * * * * * *

I see a man with a hammer and chisel chipping away at the wall in China. "As I caused the Berlin wall to fall so shall I cause the wall in China to fall. The spiritual wall will fall says the Lord."

Monday 2nd March 2009.
I saw fire on the northern shoreline of RUSSIA. From East Siberian to Laptev Sea.

"Oil is on fire, oil is on fire. It's spilled over and on fire says the Lord."

Monday 9th March 2009.
"Germany is about to erupt. Fighting in the streets and marches. They want what the government cannot give so they will retaliate."

Wednesday 11th March 2009.
Ethiopia is about to be transformed. I see a finger come down on the land of Ethiopia and presses hard so the land sinks and cracks under the pressure of the finger.

"I shake and move the land under Me says the Lord. I send a drought on Ethiopia, I send a drought on Ethiopia. Soon they will know that I am real. Soon they will know that I bless and take away blessing for I make their land parched and dry. I hold back the rain. I stop the clouds. Famine, famine, famine."

Saturday 14th March 2009.
Mozambique, I see two great hands pull a mountain apart which causes a valley between then water flows so the valley turns into a flowing river which flows with great strength and might. The two halves of mountains tries to come together again but the hand keeps them apart.

"I am about to divide your strength says the Lord to maintain stability and peace in this land. My power will flow between you so none will be greater than the other and thou you try to rebel My will will be done."

Tuesday 17th March 2009.
From the Red Sea I see clouds like smoke coming over Ethiopia. As the clouds pass over the land I see darkness being removed from off of the homes and a cleansing of the land. From the valleys to the cities there is a cleansing as the cloud moves.

* * * * * * *

France. I saw pipes running under France and they were emptying waste into the sea.

"Waste, waste, waste I will expose it."

Thursday 19th March 2009.
I see a thumb finger pressing hard into the land of Mozambique. "I press hard and deep into the land and I leave My finger print. That land knows Me says the Lord."

* * * * * * *

"Ethiopia, circumstances unseen is going to shake the land."

Sunday 22nd March 2009.
"Iran will burn says the Lord, Iran will burn. Do not doubt for you will see it."

Thursday 26th March 2009.
Romania, I see a corn tree that is planted in the ground root out of the ground and travel high into the atmosphere. It then burst out into flames and falls to the ground. But it plants itself back in the soil and it comes alive again with the blackness from the burning being removed.

"O Romania, I am rooting you up but you will be established stronger and stronger as the years go by. You have been prepared but more preparation will come as I make your soil ready for the new things."

I see the Romanian flag flying in the atmosphere but much bullets and bombs are coming at it and it falls but quickly rises again with strength.

"Nothing shall stop My will for you Romania. For you will come to life many times over."

Friday 3rd April 2009.
I saw Trinidad spinning anti clockwise and Tobago is caught up in the spinning. Out of Trinidad and Tobago comes a great light that goes up into the atmosphere and divides into many other lights that lands on various nations all over the world. The light leaves in these nations fires like campfires and bonfires.

"For out of this land other nations will have a burning, for out of this land other nations will have light, for out of this land other nations will have a gathering."

* * * * * * *

"Belgium is burning, the fields are burning. I blow My heat and the fields are burning. They will survive, quick recovery but I call My servants to the front I call My servants to authority for I have plans for Belgium and it is beyond this present day for many days will unfold and the people will seek Me for My salvation will visit."

Monday 6th April 2009.
"Many changes are coming to Ethiopia says the Lord, many changes. For I tip the scales. No more balancing act but all things will be seen."

* * * * * * *

"I trouble the islands of the Pacific. I cause them to shake and tremble. I trouble them again and again. For in the earth are many things that are not of Me and things that I scorn. What they bow to is a stench to Me and they worship the earth. So I will shake their earth says the Lord."

Tuesday 7th April 2009.
"Rioting and fighting is about to break out in South Africa. Many lives will be lost but I will have My way at the end I will have My way says the Lord. The corruption of man will spill out into the streets, wrong doing will be exposed for all to see. Look and see what I am about to do for many devils will be chased out of South Africa says the Lord."

* * * * * * *

"Cape of Good Hope. I cut deeper into the sea says the Lord."

I see ships being sucked into the sea as the water starts spinning and pulling them down.

"There are things being transported says the Lord and the waters shall claim it. Make no mistake for ships will be claimed. No accident because I see the illegal thing and I detest it so the sea will claim it."

Wednesday 8th April 2009.
"Argentina, I cause the dust to pile up on high, I cause the carcasses to reign, I cause the land to run dry. It is not coming to an end. You have been stubborn against Me so My Spirit left you. Your land is dried up. As a lion reigns so shall I reign upon the earth. As a lion roars so shill I roar in the heavens."

Sunday 12th April 2009.
I saw a dark cloud bellowing and coming up from the east over Trinidad and as it stopped over Trinidad sound mikes hung down out of the cloud and I heard: "heaven is listening."

Monday 13th April 2009.
I see a pot being stirred above the nation of Ethiopia. "I will make the nation sweet to the taste once again says God."

* * * * * * *

"Vietnam, I start a fire in Vietnam among the rich and among the poor. I send My fire to Vietnam says God."

Thursday 16th April 2009.
Ethiopia, I see a cow fall down and dies and sands of famine covers it. But then I see the sand removed and the cow comes back to life and it multiplies with other cows increasing all over the land.

"It is over says God and I restore your strength Ethiopia."

* * * * * * *

Madagascar, I see a feather in the atmosphere over Madagascar fanning the land in a north – south direction. Then the feather gently fall on the land and rest on it.

"I touch you Madagascar and gently I bring My peace, gently I bring My peace, gently I bring My peace."

* * * * * * *

"If the nations can only know Me. If the nations can only seek Me. Then what is against them will be no more. I send a word and I send a sign but many do not know Me so many do not understand. So many visitations are coming and I will shake some a little more and cause some to rise and some to fall but none will come to total ruin. My love is ever present and this is what I want them to see."

Monday 20th April 2009.
"For I roll up the nations before you says God and again I unfold them like a scroll and I show you the hidden things, the written things and the ordained things says God."

Friday 24th April 2009.
"For Venezuela will shine again. I will put a shine on them says God."
I see a white cloth shining over the land of Venezuela.

* * * * * * *

Ukraine, I see a mallet and a chisel taking away a layer of the soil and the bottom layer is dark and I hear the word: "molasses."

"I give you the sweet crops Ukraine, for I make your crops sweet."

* * * * * * *

Yugoslavia. I see two giant pieces of land that was apart and it looks as if the land was cut in half by a sharp knife. I see the two halves pressed back together.

"I heal the wounds and I make you one again Yugoslavia."

* * * * * * *

I see a rocket lunched from Ukraine but another rocket comes and blows it up in the sky.

"Be at peace, peace, peace says the Lord."

* * * * * * *

"Trinidad, I mix the colors of this land and I make the nation strong."

I see a can of paint with various colors as a rainbow being mixed in the can of paint.

"I increase you, I increase you, I increase you Trinidad."

Tuesday 28th April 2009.
While looking at the map of Brazil I saw a wooden door open in the center of the land and an eagle, scavenger and a brown dove came out.

"Three times I have freed you says God and three times I have cut you loose. For three seasons I change the atmosphere of the nation. Other nations will come to you for your substance. Your coast is rich, your coast is rich, much life is in your coast but from the center of the land great wealth is coming and you will know that I am real."

Friday 8th May 2009.
"Tunisia, I roll back the tide and I expose wealth that is hidden in the sand of your sea so dig the wealth in the sea and the liquid wealth will flow."

* * * * * * *

I see an African warrior with his shield and spear looking at a pillar (obelisk) like the one in Washington DC and the warrior is saying: "what can we do with what we have we can not beat this thing."

"For I am greater than any sign of ownership says the Lord, I am the Conqueror above all conquerors says the Lord and I break their stronghold and I free the land and no more shall you look in amazement and wonder for I will do a work."

* * * * * * *

"Afghanistan, The battles have just begun and the conflict will escalate." I see blood flowing over the land of Afghanistan.

"I visit what was done thousands of years ago and the blood still flows. A warring people are riding the waves of their fathers. Tribe against tribe, people against people the division was made and the blood still flows."

* * * * * * *

I see oriental designed ships coming to Africa from the east and casting hooks over Africa. I also see ships from the west coming and casting hooks over Africa and from the east and west end of the continent they start pulling. They peel off darkness from the continent and great light starts shining through upwards towards the sky.
I then see the continent of Africa beating as a heart beat and many white doves coming out of the heart and go all over the world, but the doves are dancing in synchronized form as they go. It looks as if they are creating music over nations as they go.

"For I cause Africa to infect the nations and affect the nations. It will happen in many seasons it will come to pass. Beyond your day the continent will burst with life and it will infect the globe."

Wednesday 13th May 2009.

I see white doves coming out of the clouds and descending on Greece. Greece is folded up as a scroll and unfolded then I see writing in Greek over the land but the understanding says: Time for a restoration, time for a new page, time for a new chapter.

"I give you a rebirth, Greece. I cause the child to come out of the womb strong and vibrant. I give you a rebirth."

****

I was looking at a map of Canada and I saw a white rose open in Canada. Three bees came out and started buzzing around the land and dropping honey on Canada.

"I will cause you to provide for yourself, I will cause you to be sustained."

Friday 15th May 2009.

"Sweden, I churn the pot and I cause your milk to be strong. You will be fed and others will receive of your milk says God. I speak life to your system, I speak life to your produce, I strengthen the weak but I punish the wrong doer who have taken advantage. The one who has used money to the pain of others I send punishment.
I make your cows fat and nourishing. I make your beef the quality of royalty. I make your milk to be sought after with great production for I give you Sweden because I remember the seeds you sowed for Me many years ago. I will not leave you hungry anymore for more is coming out of your ground and I make it rich."

****

Denmark, I see a rubix cube with various colors spinning out of control. "O Danes I am about to bring My order and My specific plan to you. Do not be afraid to break away, for with breaking away dependency is broken. Be still and all things will be in alignment, for I stop what is out of control and I slow down the uneasiness. I put My sweetness upon you. Go on ahead and produce the sweeter things."

****

"I give you another way of life Norway and I bring your strength to the surface. All is not lost and what is lost will be brought back to you at a greater measure. For many in Norway cry out to Me and I have not turned My face and I have not blocked My ear. I have seen and I have heard and I send nourishment."

I see the Spirit of God over the land of Norway and He looks like a mist.

"I come in secretly and I saturate your land and you are about to see the blessings."

* * * * * * *

"I am about to change the German mind and the German way of life. Strange things will be put in place but generations will benefit. I have not forgotten you and the old Apostles that worked for Me. The Apostles of old, the Apostles of old that came out of your land with truth on their tongue. O they labored for Me and I have not forgotten you. They sowed seeds that you do not know but I have kept watch and it is time. Be patient with change for much benefit in the future it will bring."

* * * * * * *

"Danish wealth will be exposed. They have looked for wealth in other areas but Danish wealth will be exposed."

I saw a stamp come down and stamp. God has given His stamp of approval.

* * * * * * *

"Iceland has a long journey ahead but I make the road smooth. I will carry you says God., I will carry you. I take you out of your way of doing it and I bring you into other ways says God. The ways of progress and riches. I clear the air and I cause your breath to breathe at a greater capacity. For much work is going to be done and I call you strong. And again I call you strong."

* * * * * * *

"Cush, I call you by name for many days from now I will expose the glory I will expose the splendor."

Friday 29th May 2009.
"For I open two doors to Guatemala says God. One door to enter and one door to exit. One door will soon be closed and the other will remain open for many years. For the people are involved in rituals, so I stop the external influence and I cause a new root to spring up and blossom."

I see a native Indian of Guatemala running through the land with a torch in his hand and he is setting trees and forest on fire.

"I cause the original ones to do a work for Me says God. One small fire to engulf the whole land. A fire to burn, A fire to cleanse, A fire before the new root springs up. For out of nations like these My greatness will be seen and My greatness will touch the whole earth. Many things will be changed in the house of political stronghold. Some will become weak and some will die, but I choose Guatemala as an important link between two continents to hold firm and stand strong so none will break apart."

I see a strong man with muscles holding a chain in his right hand and in his left. He is the one holding the lands together so they will not separate. The north and the south will not break apart.

"I call you strong Guatemala and I use you to maintain stability. For I give you power in the region and you will be called upon many times."

Monday 1st June 2009.
I see a wild white flower coming out of the land of France. The flower had a bee in the middle of it.

"Out of the pasture lands and the country side new moves of My Spirit and the small Church will receive the greater."

Wednesday 3rd June 2009.
Argentina, I see the land as if it is painted on canvas and a knife comes and cut the painted canvas and rips it and under the canvas are black beetles and they cover all the land of Argentina. Also fleas come out with the beetles.

"I cause a scourge to come on your land. I hand you over to the scourge."

Wednesday 17th June 2009.
In the atmosphere over France I saw twelve doors positioned in a circular fashion. Each door closed then started opening again one by one and each door represented a month of the year.

"Soon many things that were impossible will be made possible for this land."

Saturday 20th June 2009.
I see a man come out of the earth in Australia, an indigenous Australian. He then dances on the land and beautiful flowers in assortments spring up all over the land.

"I bridge the gap says the Lord and they will help each other."

* * * * * * *

I see New Zealand trembling in the sea. "Awkward things are about to happen that will bring change to a people who see things are to be done in a particular fashion but traditions can change and a new New Zealand I will cause to be born."

Thursday 25th June 2009.

Ethiopia, I see a large basket of bread on the land. The bread is coming out of the basket and going out all over the land and the bread is being eaten.

"Again I feed you says God and again I prove to you I am provider, Ethiopia."

* * * * * * *

"Eritrea, Nonsense, nonsense, nonsense I bring an end to the nonsense in your high office says God."

I see a long road as a highway through a desert with a great number of people running down the road and the more they run the road is extended.

"Man have drawn out plans that has a long ending but I expose the lies. You will see truth. Boldly I use the media and I make it strong says God. An end of the nonsense."

* * * * * * *

"St Kitts, three times I scratch your surface and the fourth time I remove the hypocrisy."

* * * * * * *

"Botswana, I make your borders strong and I make your men sturdy and I make your government unmovable says God. This is your season this is your time Botswana."

* * * * * * *

Eritrea, I see flowers like sun flowers in bloom all over the land. "After the mess, after the turmoil you will bloom."

****

"Great Brittan, I promised you a shaking and a shaking will come. I cause the sea to draw back and your hidden things will be exposed."

****

"Botswana is a great nation in hiding for I will rise up a great people. I make their hands strong, feet that cannot be moved."

I see a man in Botswana with nuggets of gold in his right hand and he says: "finally it is ours."

Monday 6th July 2009.
"Jamaica, My favor is with them and I am taking them out of dept."

****

Wednesday 8th July 2009.
"Brussels, Belgium. Soon anarchy is coming, unrest is coming but it will only be for a short time."

I see a spirit of anger in the streets grinding its teeth and growling.

"Then My water will come and wash away the unclean and the disturbance. Peace is restored but also an awakening of things that was dead."

****

"I cause the Irish to dig deep in their soil so the root will be deep and the trees will be strong. For what I am about to do will be for a generation and it must stand strong."

****

I see the city of Madrid surrounded with what looks like a white sheet and the sheet squeezes the city together. When it is released everything stays closer together.

"For I draw you as one says God and I cause you to stand as one people."

* * * * * * *

"Mississippi, I rock you and I shake you and I disturb your river. I cause over flows." I see houses being washed away by river waters. "I challenge you Mississippi and I cleanse the land."

* * * * * * *

"Earthquakes are coming, earthquakes are coming son. To the north, south, east and west earthquakes are coming. Pray for the people, pray for the nations for it is coming."

<u>Friday 31st July 2009.</u>
I see dust storms in Argentina. "I tell you Argentina is arid and dry because it symbolizes the hearts of the people." It looks as if it's a desert with dust and wind and people covered with cloth trying to make their way through.

* * * * * * *

"Russia is going to be shaken says the Lord. For they boast in many things, they beat their chest and boast in their history but its going to be shaken says the Lord. Their culture is fragmented but I will use that."

<u>Wednesday 5th August 2009.</u>
I see the surface of France being pealed off and under the earth are compartments like a maze. In one compartment I see three containers and they are leaking.

"The soil is used to keep waste but waste will not keep the soil. Tainted soil will produce tainted food." I see vegetable crops dying.

Tuesday 25th August 2009.
I see a tornado in Mexico and the tail of it is touching the Yucatan Peninsula.

"I scoop up and I bring down, I devastate and I establish for a greater work is about to be done. For I do a cleaning up and greater things will be established to benefit the people. I am still the God who cares for the people."

* * * * * * *

I see Mexico as a piece of bread and it is taken up and broken in two pieces and both pieces are eaten from. Then a great light comes and bring the two pieces as one piece of bread. The light acts as a welding that brings the two together.

"Tasty you are to Me says the Lord but better you are as one. I still the faction."

Wednesday 2nd September 2009.
"I see a clenched hand pounding on Japan. Changes, changes, changes, more changes than they can imagine."

* * * * * * *

Norway, I see a strawberry and it tears in half and a spirit in the form of a worm comes out.

"I come in deep Norway and I pull up things that you cannot see and I set you free."

Thursday 3rd September 2009.
In America I see geese flying south and they are not coming back. "Permanent changes are coming to America says the Lord."

Friday 18th September 2009.
I see a red tipped arrow in the sky pointing down at Africa. "Much blood has been spilt. I will avenge the centuries of spilt blood says the Lord for My favor is still in this place and I hold the people in high regard. But they have been lied to and while the thief had a smile on the face the hand was stealing from them and I will avenge it says God."

I see a white man with a smile on his face and his hand pulls up a blue diamond from the ground and he walks off with it hidden behind his back.

Friday 2nd October 2009.
"I will raise Ethiopia to great strength."

Monday 5th October 2009.
"Norway, I remove the shrewd man and I put a man that will do right by you."

Thursday 8th October 2009.
Eritrea, I see oil spewing out from under the desert sand. But I then see a green dragon emerge from under the same sand and the oil is spewing from a line of holes on the back of the dragon. An Angel comes and cut the head off of the dragon and it fall and dies in the sand.

"Oil production stopped, oil production stopped."

* * * * * * *

"Nigeria, I have waited and waited and I have watched all your doings. Some have become fat while others are dry. I have watched the lies and I have watched those whose lives were taken by the gun in secret and My rage is burning.

I call up the old spirits to roam your land and petrify your people." I see Nigeria being shaken and much disturbance is about to happen. "Turmoil and mayhem and the people will cry out to Me says the Lord. Those who have become fat will loose much and I am bringing a balance to the land."

Friday 9th October 2009.
Belgium, I see a market place on a street with fruits and vegetables on each side with a walkway in the middle for customers to pass through. I now see an Angel walking through the middle of the market place with its wings stretched out over the fruits and vegetables and also meats that look like pork hanging on a hook. As the wings pass over the produce and meats they turn to gold and worms come out of them and leave.

"I cleanse you Belgium. I cleanse your system, I cleanse your products, I cleanse the love of the people. It has already started and I bless your land and I purge out the things that you don't even see and greater is coming. Not much changes but what you already have will become greater says the Lord. I send My Angel and the work has begun Belgium. Do not resist. I send My favor."

* * * * * * *

Paris, I see the Effel Tower with a big red ribbon that comes and is tied half way up the tower.

"I will use your prize possession to glorify Me. Soon you will see your prize possession and see Me says the Lord."

Saturday 10th October 2009.
"Martinique, your early missionaries lied to you, they took from you." I see a big old bible and when it is open it has nothing but hollow darkness.

He Rules the Nations

I see a paint brush and it is using paint in a small glass bowl. The paint at the top of the bowl is yellow, the paint in the middle is blue and the bottom paint is green. The colors in the glass are not mixing but hold a separate place.

The brush uses the yellow paint on paper but it looks like a mess. Then it does the same with the blue and same with the green. All colors are used on the paper but no painting just a mess. With blue paint on top, green in the middle and yellow at the bottom.

"What work can I do when man is doing his own work, but I take back My brush and My hand will produce the great artwork for that land. And I will cause a great mixture in the spirit and the naked eye will see it and rejoice. I heal the old wounds Martinique."

I see the land being cleansed and washed over by crystal clear water.

"And so I will bring you about and the old influences will be no more and the things planted will be removed as I bring Martinique to the place of substance."

I see a hand spin Martinique and its spinning rapidly in a clockwise direction.

"Quick advancement and quick referrals. I develop you quickly and quickly old things are removed."

I see the clear water still doing a work on the land and dark wood stakes are coming from under the soil and leaving the land. I see the old bible closed and swiftly removed out of the vision.

"It is finished," says God, "It is finished."

* * * * * * *

I see a hand with a pencil draw a line across the top of Florida. Florida then brakes off and floats towards the south and joins with Cuba.

"All things are possible with Me," says God, "for in future times when the time is right a union will be made. I will unify the people, the families and the sons and daughters will know each other once again," says God, "Resolutions will be made, distant things will be brought near. Quickly I do a work and quickly the work is finished."

Thursday 22nd October 2009.
Belgium, I see a trap door of a wood floor open and an eight ball from the game of pool rolls down and go deep into the soil and hits a row of white balls.

"I remove old promises," says God, "but I renew the strength of the land as I take you deep and I show you good things. I take away the two most important balls of the game and I make it all even for everyone. This is your day of reckoning, this is the day My hand comes down and searches, this is the day I take the stick and play the balls as I choose," says God.

I see a man take the pool stick and plays pool by hitting the balls without any eight ball or white ball.

Thursday 29th October 2009.
Belgium, I see a page in the spirit with writing on it: "I give them a new constitution, a new law, a new way of life."

Friday 30th October 2009.
Belgium, I see a tightly closed fist with a rolled up piece of paper in it. "I hold in My hand," says God, "the writings for this nation, the directions for this nation, the future work of this nation."

Thursday 3rd November 2009.
Belgrade, I see a field of red roses with yellow flowers between them. The red roses are opening up and the yellow flowers are blushing and smiling. The yellow flowers start swaying and singing together: "All is well, all is well", over and over again.

"For season after season," says God, "I will mushroom your land. Pleasing things are coming and times of peace. You will even taste it in the atmosphere. Even the Church that is sleeping will come alive and a fresh scent will take the land. Be open, be expectant, times of blossoming are coming Belgrade, greater things are at your doorsteps."

* * * * * * *

Yugoslavia, I see the middle finger of a hand touch the land. "Three times I touch your land," says God, "and barren things will come alive and give birth to greater things. One touch and I will shake the land, another touch and it will come alive and another touch the birthing of things you longed for. Yugoslavia My hand is ready."

Friday 6th November 2009.
"Belgium will rise to great strength I will make the economy a strong arm."

Monday 30th November 2009.
Belgium, I see snow falling on the land then a bottle of blue ink is in the atmosphere above the land. I see the ink is suctioned out of the bottle and one drop of ink is dropped on the land and the whole land is saturated with ink. All the snow on the land becomes blue. Then more drops of ink falls on the land until the bottle of ink is empty and the ink saturates deep into the earth. I see the ink going deep into the Belgian soil.

"I will saturate you," says God, "but not the way you expect it. I will boost your economy and cause life to burst from your people. I remove the coldness from the heart and I saturate, and I saturate, and I saturate."

Monday 7th December 2009.
I see a cutlass cut off the clock tower of Big Ben in London then it cuts off one of the towers at Buckingham Palace.

"Soon one will be taken away and then another will be taken. I cut down their royalty," says God, "I cut down their royalty. I take away the pillar and I cause confusion. I am the One that puts up and the One that cuts down. But the one coming shall be worst than the last."

* * * * * * *

Bonn, Germany. I see an Angel mixing colors in a tin of paint and he is using a stick. The colors are blue, yellow and white. The Angel then takes a taste of the paint.

"Hum, this is good. They will know the mixture of God. I put all things as one and blend."

Thursday 10th December 2009.
I see Spain being flipped in a frying pan as you would flip pancakes. Then I see many other nations being flipped in frying pans.

"They believe they have rule over themselves, but I am still God of all the earth and I will allow nothing to happen before its time and without My commands. Many believe they have the answer but they will go around in circles unless they seek Me. They are being tossed around and they have no true answers, but some think they have the answer and many lies are spoken and the earth is deceived. Truth is coming and the heat will increase for I am in control."

* * * * * * *

Jerusalem, Jerusalem, Jerusalem. I see a green leaf up in the atmosphere and great light is hitting it and pushing it forward.

"Many times I have called you Jerusalem and you have not listened. Many times I want to flourish you and endow you, but you were not ready.
I still call you My own, I still call you My city, I still call you My people. Listen Jerusalem and you will hear Me."

Wednesday 16th December 2009.
France, I see a man with a pickaxe digging a straight line in the soil and he is an oriental looking man with a broad hat. He digs so deep that he hit a buried canister and it look like gas is released. He then drops the pickaxe and run away.

"Who you brought in to do your work can eventually work against you says God."

* * * * * * *

"The German tongue shall change, their language shall change, there way of life shall change."

* * * * * * *

I see Germany being turned over a fire as if you would roast meat. "I am making them well done," says the Lord, "well done."

* * * * * * *

Martinique, I see a rope between Martinique and France. On the Martinique end a man is holding the rope and on the France end a man is holding the rope. They are pulling as if it's a tug of war and they are both putting everything they have into pulling until the man on Martinique side gives a great pull and gains most of the rope from France.

"The struggle will be won; I give the smaller the victory over the greater."

* * * * * * *

"Ecuador, many challenges and dependencies but I will soon show you how rich you are and I will teach you how to manage your riches."

* * * * * * *

"New York, New York, New York you will loose your luster you will loose your pride. Your injustice is against you."

Thursday 31st December 2009.
I see a jet black stallion horse come out of the desert sands in Saudi Arabia and the eyes of the horse is red and both back legs are crippled. It still has the ability to circle the land by riding along the border of Saudi Arabia.

"I have shown you the spirit of that land. The rear legs of the horse is broken because of dependency on another country but the horse is still moving along."

Monday 4th January 2010.
I saw the black stallion of Saudi Arabia and this time it spoke and said: "Release my legs another nation have a hold on my legs."

Monday 11th January 2010.
Eritrea, I see a yellow flower blooming. It look like a sunflower. "Nothing shall stop My work in you, nothing shall stop what I am about to do for in your land dwell spirits of anarchy but I root out and I bring good things among you."

I see many white flowers also blooming. "I bring you to the stage of age and maturity

Eritrea. I make your feet strong and your arm strong. Don't look back for the greater is coming. It's already planted in the land and undiscovered but in time discoveries will be made and you will harvest. Greater things are coming Eritrea, greater things are coming."

* * * * * * *

Djibouti, I see a snake like dragon come out of your sand and it goes up and eat the moon then it falls to the ground dead.

"Never again will I permit another god. For I am all that I say that I am and no other god shall rise against Me."

Sunday 17th January 2010.
Brussels, I see a big yellow flower opening up in bloom. "I open you up and I cause the greater to be exposed. You will be a sweet fragrance."

Friday 22nd January 2010.
Egypt, I see a man in the atmosphere above you and he is dressed as they would dress in the desert with his head banded, beard and long covering. He is holding over the land a white sheet and in the top left hand corner is a green crescent moon and star.
He then rests the sheet on the land of Egypt and it sinks into the land. Then he rides off on a horse up in the spirit and says: "Woe to that land for a great earthquake is coming."

Tuesday 26th January 2010
Germany, I see a pancake flopped on one side and being burnt on the side that is facing the fire.

"I burn one portion of their history, for many live in another Germany in their minds. Many still see two Germanys and live that way but I burn away one portion so only one Germany can be seen."

* * * * * * *

"Curacao, The waters, the waters, I still the waters. Some of their waters are dirty and polluted but I pass over and refresh. I come in deep and I cause hidden things to come to the surface. Curacao I am coming, Curacao I am coming."

* * * * * * *

Qatar, I see an upside down tornado over a refinery and it is pulling the refinery up so the refinery is getting taller and stronger.

"I visit Qatar; I visit and strengthen what they already have."

Saturday 13th February 2010.
While in prayer about Haiti and voodoo God opened my eyes to see a bigger picture. The Roman Catholic priest and leadership in Haiti are great perpetrators of voodoo practices and witchcraft. They work along with voodoo priest and priestesses. They have an underground location where they will meet and work together.
I saw Roman Catholic Priest getting women pregnant, paying them for the babies and then using the babies for sacrifices.
I saw a baby and a knife cutting the baby down the middle from the neck through the center of the chest down the belly to the private parts. The other cut is made across the chest so a cross is cut into the baby as it is sacrificed.

Thursday 18th February 2010.
I see a scroll with writing on it come down on Greece and a man which represents the whole land he is awaken as a man awakes in the morning after sleep. People lay down placards and the anger is gone. They now rejoice dancing and singing in the streets.

"Greece I give you a new day, a new constitution. I turn it around for you. I have not forgotten, I still recognize you, receive My favor."

Saturday 20th February 2010.
"Bridgetown Barbados is about to be rocked."

<u>Monday 1st March 2010.</u>
"Israel have fallen, the prince of Israel have fallen. Earthquakes and storms are coming. Israel have fallen."

* * * * * * *

"Belgium will receive the breeze of My anointing. I see a great hand lift Belgium out of the soil and bring it up."

* * * * * * *

I see Kuwait moved a little to the west. "I make new friends for that land for what I have planned for them will be accomplished."

* * * * * * *

Belize, O Belize. I see Jesus take up Belize and hold it in His bosom as a mother comforts a child.

"I will mother you Belize, I will mother you. I will give you from my breast and a new maturity is coming."

* * * * * * *

I see Bermuda and the triangle. "Soon the great lie will be exposed. The great lie of man will be exposed."

* * * * * * *

O Belize. I see Belize in the bosom of Jesus and it is growing quickly and rapidly from a baby to a full man, strong with muscles.

"You will no longer be dependant as a baby but I will bring you to maturity, I will make you strong, I will make you stand. Much influence I give you Belize, much influence I give you."

* * * * * * *

Sri Lanka, Sri Lanka, Sri Lanka. I see a Muslim man dressed in white with a white head piece and he has a rifle which is taking careful aim and firing. But the mouth of the rifle melts and then the whole gun melts out of his hand.

"I take it away from them. In Sri Lanka I take it away from them."

Tuesday 2nd March 2010.
"The islands are about to be shaken son. I am going to disturb the economy; I am going to disturb the governments. Things that are in place will fall out of place but a new dawn, a new day, a new development for new strength and purpose. Look again."

When I first looked I saw the islands shaking in the Caribbean Sea but this time I saw flowers coming out of the islands and blossoming in various colors of white, yellow, blue, green, red, pink and other colors. Some flowers are big and some small coming out of the soil of the islands and reaching up to the sky. I see rays of light from the sky coming down on the flowers and the face of the flowers are smiling in the light and singing:

"Now we rise, now we shine, we worship the Divine
We have been shaken, we have experienced darkness
But now we rise; now we shine
We worship Jesus the Divine."

* * * * * * *

"Martinique, your freedom has come. Martinique, your time have come. I break the chains."

I see the hands of a man in chains but then he pulls them apart and they are broken.

"You will survive Martinique. I will not give you freedom for you to fail, you will survive. Do not fear for your children for My strength is with them."

Monday 8th March 2010.
I saw Egypt turned upside down with the bottom part of the earth facing up. I see men in white with white caps and rifles in their hands running toward the leader to assassinate.

"I cause overthrow, I cause upheaval in that land. Many warnings have been given but no heed so now I move."

Isaiah 19:2-4. "I will set Egyptians against Egyptians; everyone will fight against his brother, and everyone against his neighbor, City against city, kingdom against kingdom. The spirit of Egypt will fail in its midst; I will destroy their council, and they will consult the idols and the charmers, the mediums and the sorcerers. And the Egyptians will give into the hands of a cruel master, and a fierce king will rule over them," Says the Lord, the Lord of host. Nkjv.

Thursday 18th March 2010.
Ecuador, I see a strainer sifting sand and some little black bolts that look like coal coming out of the sifting.

"I sift your sands Ecuador and the little thing will amount to much. For I take you out of dependency on others and give you a leader with My vision and purpose who will remove the blanket of lies and you will see the goodness that is in you, that is in your land. Many other hidden things I will expose for your benefit and the benefit of your children and the stability of your land.

Beware of the cows that eat too much for they will eat from your land and get fat off of you. Much is about to be exposed. I give you My sovereignty, and be blessed land I have chosen, be blessed."

Wednesday 7th April 2010.
"Egypt, transformation is coming to Egypt."

* * * * * * *

"Morocco shall fall." I see a mountain range torn apart and slammed back together three times until the mountain and its ranges crumble and fall apart into the sea.

Friday 9th April 2010.
I see a big sea shell sprinkling gold dust on the islands of the far east. The shell is above the islands and sprinkling as it moves. The shell then brakes and falls into the sea. One broken part fall into the North Pacific and the other into the South Pacific. It causes growth in sea life because fishes, mammals and octopuses are growing larger than normal.

"I bring growth to the islands to the far east. A growth that will not be hindered and what is established in the spirit will not be stopped because I ordain a processing for them where they will establish greater things in time. I build them, I establish them, I strengthen them and bring their states to maturity. Keep watch over them son, keep watch over them and you will see the greater things happen. What you see happening in the physical is not a deterrent so see what I am doing in the islands."

I see a chain linking all the islands and the linking is happening quickly. The links of the chain is growing as if it has life in it and the islands are also growing big and healthy looking. They beat as a heart would beat and I hear the word: "Increase."

* * * * * * *

I see an ink roller rolling over Memphis, Tennessee. It is rolling and throwing down the buildings and rolling blue ink on Memphis.

Thursday 15th April 2010.
I see a great hand take Denmark and squeeze it together and it turns into dough. The hand then kneads the dough.

"I am making you over Denmark. New things are about to happen. Three new governments and each fulfilling a specific purpose for Me."

* * * * * * *

"Justice will prevail in the United Nations. Some breakdowns and some exposures but justice will prevail in the United Nations."

* * * * * * *

I see Jamaica turning in the sea then it turns into a water wheel but as the water wheel turns it throws water on Florida and Florida looks as if it is a man waking up from a night sleep.

"Yes Jamaica I will use you to help a greater land. I will use your substance to bring life."

* * * * * * *

I see Martinique as a child blowing bubbles in the sea. "Time to get serious," says the Lord, "for I am about to bring you to maturity. You will govern yourself. I am about to bring you to maturity says the Lord."

* * * * * * *

I see the buildings in Jerusalem bending over to the right side because a strong wind as a storm is pushing from the left. Some of the big buildings are rooted up and blown away but the smaller buildings as houses are left. They have flames of fire in them but the houses are not consumed.

"The things that try to be bigger than Me I remove," says God, "but the humble will receive from Me. I start little fires in Jerusalem but all will connect. Each fire have a specific purpose for I will start by cleansing the families and I bring the homes back to Me. Little do they know that I am in the midst of them and I have searched the land and I have chosen the homes. I still love you Jerusalem."

I see a white sheet that looks like a silk cloth come down from the sky and rest gently on Jerusalem. As I look into Jerusalem I see dark shadows, snakes and dark deformed looking creatures leaving homes and marching out of Jerusalem. They look like ants marching and they go into the sea, into the deepest parts of the sea.

"I free you," says God, "I cleanse the homes and I free you. But I also call you back to My face which is light so the dark things cannot return. I have bound many for you Jerusalem but you keep calling them back. Again I free you."

Friday 16th April 2010.
"Ecuador will have many doors open to them. They have tried many times and failure came their way but now My favor have come and growth and sustainability will be established for a future generation that will hear my voice. I choose you Ecuador and I will show you My new ways," says God. "I have seen past injustice and you thought I wasn't looking but I know all things and My judgment is specific and does not miss the mark. So as I open doors for you Ecuador. I lift you up and I clean you off and I bring old things to pass for greater things are about to happen."

* * * * * * *

Paris, I see the Eiffel Tower and it brakes at the base on the left side. I then see the tower bending to the left and it is a giant man in the spirit who has a rope attached to the top of the tower and this giant man in the spirit with a smile is pulling the rope and bending the tower to the left. But then an Angel comes and cut the rope and the tower returns to its up right position and the base that was broken is healed and restored.

"You were led astray but I will restore you. I also heal the broken people. Many pains and misfortunes will be cleaned up. I come in and I set apart and I distinguish right from wrong and I make all things peaceful. Stand again Paris, stand again."

* * * * * * *

"Ecuador will be transformed, Ecuador will be transformed."

Wednesday 28th April 2010.
"Jerusalem is about to be shaken son, it is about to be shaken. I will shake the mountain top. I shall shake the base. The trees and even the rocks. And the strength of the land shall be shaken."

Sunday 16th May 2010.
New Zealand, I see a young golden brown dog lying on a small mat. It looks like a sheep dog. It is looking at me and panting, waging its tail and smiling. It then gets angry and growls at me, then it returns to the state of panting, waging its tail and smiling.

"Many times they wanted the sheep to come home but the stock was low. But now I answer their prayer and much work is coming for I increase their stock. What was small I multiply it and what was multiplied I increase. I make their stock fat and healthy. I give their stock world wide acceptance."

* * * * * * *

Wichita, Kansas. I see a tornado hitting a red barn but the barn is not destroyed or moved. The tornado keep hitting it but nothing happens, not even a scratch. A mouth in the tornado then breathes on the barn and it falls over and crumbles into pieces of wood.

"What seems to be strong will eventually crumble, Kansas."

Saturday 29th May 2010.
"Uganda have a fire for Me. I will eventually burn the nations around them. There will be an outpouring and infecting. The fire in Uganda is a great flame of My Spirit and out of the heart of Africa will raise a nation that had great turmoil and shame.
I take away the shame and I take away the resentment and I pour in My Spirit. I raise up the ministers and lay man with a difference. The ones that will do it with much difference and accomplish much for Me in the heart of Africa."

I see Uganda burning and then the nations around them also burning. I see giant worms coming out of the fire and leaving. I hear rejoicing with music and singing. I hear the word "rejoice", "rejoice", being shouted.

Sunday 30th May 2010.
Trinidad and Tobago. I see blood flowing out of the Red House and flowing down Fredrick Street, Chacon Street and St Vincent Street. I see dark spirits of mayhem running about in the street putting fear in the people.

"Soon, soon, soon blood will flow, soon; soon, soon it will come crashing down". I then saw the Prime Ministers residence and something that look like fireworks went up into the air then fell on the residence and the house burned and came crashing down.

I saw a giant blue snake with some orange color on it come out of the collapsed house. It had a wound on the head and on the lower part. It went to the Queens Park Savannah and died their.

"Soon I say son, soon". I prayed: "Let your will be done in this nation Lord but I will not like any of my people to lose their lives." "This is what they asked for son this is what they wanted."

Tuesday 22nd June 2010.
Belgium. I see a sash come down from the sky. "I wrap you says God in My goodness, I wrap you says God in My favor."

* * * * * * *

St Kitts, I see a great big hand lift the island out of the sea and a voice said: "Look what the Lord can do with the littlest of nations. I am about to prove who I am by using this small island and the world will know not to despise the little because greatness is coming to them and I do it soon. Soon St Kitts will be exalted."

* * * * * * *

"Jamaica, stop the rebellion against Me, stop the rebellion against Me. I want to clean you up."

* * * * * * *

Barbuda, I see a big face blow away a dark cloud from over Barbuda. "I cleanse your atmosphere, I cleanse your shore."

* * * * * * *

"Seven times I touch Trinidad and Tobago but this time I come in hard. This time there is blood shed. I come in hard, I come in hard."

* * * * * * *

"Belgium will burst out with great rejoicing. Rejoicing is coming to Belgium."

* * * * * * *

I see in the atmosphere above Madagascar a man with a turban on his head releasing a snake on Madagascar but a great sword comes and cut off the head of the snake.

"The sorcery will stop. No more tolerance for the sorcery."

* * * * * *

I see a hand with a hacksaw cutting off the top part of England and then the part that was cut off is eaten.

"This is tasty to Me, they have done well, they have done well."

* * * * * *

I see Madagascar being bent and it brakes in two pieces. "Their breaking is coming, I will break the land, I will divide them greatly."

Sunday 25th July 2010.
I looked into Iran and I saw the nation shaking as an earthquake would shake it and then the nation cracked in half. Then the Lord said: "It is finished, it is done, it is finished."

Sunday 29th August 2010.
"Much fighting will begin in Iraq. The tribes come together but they will separate and fight. The start of war, the start of another war."

* * * * * *

"Justice, justice, justice. I call Iran to justice."

* * * * * *

I see Sweden wrapped in a white cloth as a baby would be wrapped. The north western part of Sweden was not wrapped but exposed symbolizing the face of the baby but the rest of the land was wrapped in the white cloth.

"Sweden, do you think I have forgotten. I will comfort you. I remember your hard work and I will comfort you. Rest assured."

Tuesday 7th September 2010.
I see the north east region of Australia break off from the rest of the land and drift east. "This is not devastation," says the Lord, "but I give them expansion. I expand their influence, I expand their territory. I give them great expansion."

* * * * * * *

Ukraine, I see two soldiers in world war one uniforms and they were opposite each other. The one on the left had a red uniform and the one on the right had a green uniform. They both rushed towards each other to fight but the soldier in the green uniform wins because the red uniform ends up on the ground and the soldier in green kills him by wounding him in the neck with his knife which is attached to the rifle.

"Many old things still hold the people. Pain and disappointment but soon, and I say soon, I shall move over the land."

I see two Angels holding a white sheet and moving it over the land and the sheet is scooping up what looks like black smoke and Ukraine look as if it is covered in snow and cleansed.

"I change the season and I change the time and I am coming in Ukraine, I am coming in. Your weather will change which will signify change that is already beginning in the spirit. I also break dependency and you will stand."

* * * * * * *

Latvia, I see the chest of a woman open and I can see her heart beating. The heart is strong and muscular. I then see the chest closed up and many are being breast fed. Many are coming to this woman to be breast fed.

"Latvia you are stronger than you think and you will feed thousands."

* * * * * * *

"Spain, justice is served, My justice is served."

* * * * * * *

Lithuania, I see a man in a business suit trying to load ammunition in a large military gun but he looks odd and the ammunition doesn't look right.

"Many are in the wrong place and position but I will put each man in the right place and function for smooth transferal and no obstacles."

Saturday 25th September 2010.
"A worship will come out of Africa that the world have never seen. It will compass the earth and many will be consumed in My glory."

Wednesday 6th October 2010.
"I have measured Taiwan and found them wanting. I have measured Taiwan and found them doing things under the table. I have measured Taiwan and its time for a breaking. It is the season for Taiwan's breaking. One season breaking, another season restoration. My Church have liberty so My favor is with them."

Sunday 10th October 2010.
I saw a strange looking weapon cut Turkey in half from north to south, Black Sea to Mediterranean. One of the halves drifted a little towards the west.

Note: The weapon I saw was a rod about six feet long with a blade at the end and the blade was about one foot long and slightly curved. On my research I found out it was a weapon used by the Huns and in ancient China it was called a "Guan Dao." It might have also been used by the Moguls and the Japanese call it a "Naginata."

"I am forming new ties, I am making new links says the Lord. Centuries ago invaders came and their spirit still linger. I am cutting the past to make new ties. I am making new friends for you Turkey, new affiliations."

I see a white cloud come from the east and pass through Turkey and the land look as if silver dust has been sprinkled over it because there is a glitter.

Sunday 7th November 2010.
I see Argentina spinning. "I spin you around Argentina and I make old things new. I take away the pain I take away the cloud of sadness. The mindsets will change and I cause the people to have one mind for My purpose. I will bring you out as a strong baby vibrant and ready. Old gone, new have come."

Saturday 20th November 2010.
"Man shall walk on the moon again and discover new things. The dust that heals."

Sunday 21st November 2010.
"San Andres fault shall shake and tremble and many lives shall be lost. But I will unify the people and they will help each other and they will love each other. It is coming son it is coming."

Monday 29th November 2010.
"I see a giant clenched fist from the sky and it is pounding on Pakistan."

Monday 6th December 2010.
"Iran is about to be judged son. It is about to happen."

Sunday 12th December 2010.
Guatemala, I see from the Pacific Ocean to the Caribbean Sea darkness as a canopy comes from the seas and joins over the nation.

It then slams down on the nation three times. I then see something that look live silver exposed in the nation.

"Much things that are hidden will be exposed Guatemala. Hardships will cause precious things to come to the forefront. Lives will be lost but a generation will live Guatemala, a generation will live."

* * * * * * *

Beirut, I see a small palm tree in the desert. "You will stand alone, you will not come to another level of maturity, you will not come to full strength."

Tuesday 14th December 2010.
I see a white worm come out of the earth in Mexico. It goes into the Caribbean Sea and swims over to Cuba. It goes into the earth of Cuba with the head on the surface and it said: "I will rest here for a while until my time comes and I will show them my power."

"O Cuba I am about to shake you from in your earth. I see cracks in the Cuban soil. I am bringing change from beneath and I will cause your island to shake and tremble."

* * * * * * *

Jerusalem, Jerusalem, Jerusalem. I see Israel as a sheet of white paper. The paper is then rolled up as a scroll with a red ribbon tied as a bow around it holding it together.

Saturday 25th December 2010.
I see Florida and on the map I see Tallahassee burning. "I am burning through and through this place. I am burning through."

Monday 3rd January 2011.
"Earthquakes are coming to Ethiopia, son, earthquakes are coming. I shall shake the land, I shall sift the soil, earthquakes are coming."

Monday 17th January 2011.
Paris, I see the Eiffel Tower bend to the left and bend to the right then straighten up again.

"Some will be bent and some will be straightened but I will have My way in this city. There are some who know Me and there are those who disregard Me but I will rule in this city. O romantic place, o romantic house I will rule in you. I have already taken up My position and the right wing is bending and the left wing is bending. Who have to be bent will be bent because I rule and I will have My way.
I will prove to you that I am still God and My Son's voice must not be stopped. I will prove to you that I am real and not to be taken likely. Paris I am coming and who dare to stop Me."

* * * * * * *

Ecuador, I see a mountain part and divide in two then a giant serpent moves between the parted mountain.

"When division comes the enemy will come in, keep your eyes open Ecuador keep your eyes open. He is looking for an opportunity and when he gets it he will keep you divided. Keep your eyes open O nation, keep your eyes open."

* * * * * * *

Paris, I see the Eiffel Tower jump out of place and starts dancing in the streets. "I will give you great rejoicing Paris, not many years from now, I will give you great rejoicing; It is coming."

Tuesday 18th January 2011.
"Atlanta, Georgia will be shaken. The buildings are coming down and lives will be lost. Pray for them son, pray for them."

Monday 31st January 2011.

Germany, I see people in the streets and it looks like rejoicing and joy as they hold a piece of white paper in their hand.

"Much jubilation is coming as I visit that land and bring change. Ratification and transformation. Restructuring of daily lives. I am coming in Germany, I am coming in."

* * * * * * *

Denmark, I see a boat on the shore. "I am pushing you out into deeper things. You will not stand on the shore and watch other boats go out but you are about to go out and you will be a leader on particular matters. Yes, restructuring and accomplishment all for My glory. The greater is about to happen Denmark, the greater."

* * * * * * *

"I will sing you a song Sweden and it will tantalize you and mesmerize you where you will forget the issues of life. What was once hard I will make it easy for you to accomplish."

* * * * * * *

"Denmark, the old days are gone."

* * * * * * *

Brisbane, I see a ring of fire surrounding Australia. I see what looks like dark smoke and ashes falling from the sky towards Australia, but a dome covers Australia and what falls from the sky hits the dome and disappears.

"Australia is secure says God, Australia is secure."

* * * * * * *

"Guadeloupe, ha, ha, ha you think it won't happen? I will make you independent. O yes I will, and I will teach you how to take care of yourself. Many visitations are coming, many."

* * * * * * *

"Danes are about to rejoice, the Danes are about to rejoice."

* * * * * * *

I see an old fashioned pot cooking on a camp fire. "A little of this and a little of that I put in the pot to make Germany sweeter."

* * * * * * *

"Albuquerque, New Mexico. The old flag still flies in the atmosphere, but I bring it down and now, peace."

* * * * * * *

"Grace, at this time, in this day I give grace to Australia."

* * * * * * *

Lithuania, I see a knife being sharpened the old fashioned way on a strap of leather. But then the knife is tossed.

"I do away with your old way Lithuania and in times and seasons I make you better."

* * * * * * *

Bonn, Germany, I see a man in an old fashioned German uniform. Black pants, red top, red hat and he is on a white horse.

"Make no mistake Germany I will deal with your pride, I will deal with your pride."

Tuesday 1st February 2011.
"Egypt will fall soon; the power of Egypt will fall."

* * * * * * *

"My sun will shine on Ethiopia and when it does I will cause great rejoicing in Ethiopia this year. Their will be great rejoicing in Ethiopia this year."

Monday 7th February 2011.
"Buckingham Palace is about to be shaken. I am about to shake Buckingham Palace to the foundation. Yes, yes, yes this is a true word too the foundation will be shaken. I will expose what is deep; I will expose what is hidden.
You will see the shaking, you will see the shaking. It is a sure thing. No Kingdom is greater than Me and who ever lifts up their horn against Me will be broken, their horn will be broken. It is done already son. It is already fixed."

Tuesday 22nd February 2011.
I keep seeing Barbados in the spirit. "I am about to bring it out of dark things. I am about to shift the land. The people will be shaken and their hearts will fail but after this occurrence I bring a new island to the forefront."

* * * * * * *

"You know New Zealand has been shaken but I have just begun because I will shake their way of life. Stubborn, stubborn, stubborn people I will shake their way of life for the new season and the new nation to come out. O what a great glory from a far away land. They will honor Me. Great glory will come out of them especially in government and other high places."

* * * * * * *

"Another storm is coming to Grenada but this time it is a spiritual storm. You will hear of great revival."

Sunday 27th February 2011.
"Belize, much is given, much is under the earth. I will cause them to reap; I will cause them to pull up. For they will receive great things from their own soil."

I see a diamond come out of the soil and it is spinning in the atmosphere. "Belize, Belize believe and you will see the greater."

Monday 28th February 2011.
"I see Argentina being flipped in a frying pan. They must know that I am God; they must know that I am real. I make them fat again, I make them edible."

* * * * * * *

"Iraq, many seeds of discord has been planted. America has lied. The sword of Iran has been sharpened."

Saturday 12th March 2011.
I see a man in France dressed in the French football uniform. He kicked the ball and it landed in Spain and into the Spanish goal. The French player said: "Next time the victory is ours for sure."

Monday 14th March 2011.
"Mozambique will receive My wrath soon but then a new sunrise, a new day, a new chapter, a reconstruction. I am working in all things and I allow many things for My purposes. A new day is coming for Mozambique but first turmoil."

* * * * * * *

Madagascar, I see a star fall from the sky and land in the sea east of Madagascar. "The waters will come raging towards you Madagascar but I will slow it down before it hits you. Not much damage, not many will be lost. My grace is still on the earth; My grace is still on the earth."

* * * * * * *

"Charleston, West Virginia, A major uproar that will affect the whole nation." I see a waterfall over that state and the water is falling on West Virginia. "I will fall on you and use you to bring great change."

* * * * * * *

"Mississippi, watch out I am coming down against you, I will hit your water and it will come against you, watch out."

* * * * * * *

"America must know I am about to hit their pride and I am coming down hard."

Wednesday 16th March 2011.
Ecuador, I see a book with empty pages. A hand with a feather pen start writing on the pages and it is writing fast.

"Fast I do a work in you Ecuador, fast I establish you Ecuador, fast I do a revolution in Ecuador."

* * * * * * *

"Jamestown. The massacre, the massacre. The blood is not dry on the land. I still smell it. I know what really happened says the Lord and My vengeance is sure, sure, sure, sure. I see all, I know all, I am God."

* * * * * * *

He Rules the Nations

Martinique, I see a demonic spirit in the atmosphere above Martinique, and it is enticing Martinique saying: "Stay with the French it is better for you because you cannot make it on your own."

"Lies, lies, lies he is a great liar," says God. "Church in Martinique rise and fight. Release your arrows. Take careful aim and it will come down. Move quickly Church, speedily, waste no time. Your nation must be moved out of the clutches. I want to make a union with the islands. Greater things are in store for this region, greater things for My pleasure. I will rejoice, greater things."

* * * * * * *

Ecuador, I see what looks like a caveman with a club and he is over Ecuador. He is frozen in one position. "He is waiting for My orders, Now go."

I see the caveman hitting the land and it is shaking. He then rests for a time and starts hitting the land again but it looks as if he is doing it playfully.

"I know how to deal with this people; I know how to get them where I want them."

* * * * * * *

I see black footprints, starting in Venezuela and traveling across the northern part of South America through Central America, up to Mexico and stop at the border of America.

"The invasion will not enter. Those spirits are not allowed to enter. I have closed the door in their face. This time I stand guard for America, this time."

* * * * * * *

The building which the clock "Big Ben" is attached to, British Parliament. I see a cutlass in the hand of a giant Angel and the Angel is violently chopping the building and it is trembling and crumbling, falling apart.

"I rule," says God, "they must know that I rule."

* * * * * * *

"Martinique, if you try harder, just a little effort and I will give you the victory." I see a man on the beach in a beach chair. He has on sun glasses and he is relaxing.

"Get out of that position," says God, "and start the fight again. Victory is given, victory is given, victory is given."

* * * * * * *

I see a fat, big belly oriental man with the word China written on his belly. He is moving forward but has many problems carrying his big belly. His cheeks are puffing and he is sweating. He collapses on his belly because of the weight and pressure of carrying it.

"They have over worked the man, they have over worked the man and the man will collapse."

Thursday 17th March 2011.
Ghana, I see a black man in a white baseball uniform with red pin stripes and a red cap on his head. The cap has a "C" on it and he also has a baseball bat in his hand.

"I will export the game and greater players will come forth."

Friday 18th March 2011.
Mexico, I see a hand peal the surface off of the land and under the surface is a nest of giant white worms.

"I expose what is hidden, My fire will expose it."

* * * * * * *

In France I see a tall metal tower with a radio antenna at the top. It is broadcasting and the signal is going out. I see "Air France". The tower then looks as if it is alive and it swings to the right, then to the left. It then walks into the sea and sinks but the red light at the top of the tower is a little above the surface of the water and the broadcasting signal is still going out.

"Greater things are coming, a wider scope and greater influence."

* * * * * * *

In Germany, I see God peal off the surface of the earth in the north eastern region. "I see you; I see your hidden things. I want you to know Germany that I see you."

* * * * * * *

"Red Cross, return to your original intention or I will expose you. O yes Red Cross know for sure I will expose you."

* * * * * * *

Over Germany, I see a great hand with a pouch in it. The pouch is opened and shiny silver balls are falling out of the pouch and landing on Germany and rolling over the land. The balls are so heavy it looks as if they are making ditches.

"I create new ways of doing things, new emphasis, new laws."

* * * * * * *

I see tomatoes on a conveyer belt and they are falling into boxes for shipping. One box is filled and moves off and I see Germany over it. Another box is filled and I see Toronto over it.

"Both boxes have the same products son, but they are going different places. I will sustain them, I will nourish them, I will keep them."

* * * * * * *

Brussels, I see a flag pole with a white flag on it and the pole is on the ground. It is then raised up again with the white flag flying high. Spots of blood are splashed on the flag but the rain washes it off. Spots of blood are splashed on the flag again and wind and rain washes it off. The flag is then lowered and someone takes it and runs off with it and I hear: "Hurray we win."

"I remove the disguise and I will show what is really happening."

Sunday 20th March 2011.
"A rising in Ethiopia, a rising in Ethiopia."

Monday 21st March 2011.
Belize, I see the dark image of a person and a cutlass cuts off the hands of the person.

"I stop the rituals and I stop the dirty hands and I wash the land. You have rebelled against Me with your ancestral worship but My plans will be fulfilled and My work will be done. More missionaries are coming, more missionaries are coming and even the government will listen.
Don't you know I have been watching you for centuries and even before the man came across the sea? And what I destine will come to pass and My will will flourish." says the Most High God.

I see bamboo sticks stuck in the ground with images of faces on the top of it.

"This is what you put before Me. This is what you worship. I will wash them away and show you My strength, with a breadth they will fall. You say Christianity have no power but Belize I am coming in and you will receive power. This is what the Lord says and so you will know, so you will know My plans are great but I must clean the land. I must clear the way for My plan to flourish. I am coming in Belize I am coming in."

I see the image of a strong muscular man marching across the sea and marching into Belize.

* * * * * * *

Jamaica, Jamaica, Jamaica. I see a feather slowly and gently falling from the sky and resting on Jamaica.

"I give you My peace and you have rejected it. Again I give you peace. Soon it will rest on you. I am putting people in place in Jamaica people who know Me. You will hear about it son you will hear about those in high position who know Me. The work have already begun and it will be finished. I am taking back the land. It is Mine says God."

* * * * * * *

St Kitts, I see a giant dark demon over you and like a vacuum its mouth is sucking up your money. But I hear the word "stop" and everything stops. Even the money stops in mid air and not even the demon can move. I hear the words, rage and anger, over and over again.

"This thing was sent to do harm to this people. Those on the outside sent it but I will put a stop to it."

* * * * * * *

"Many lodges will fall, many lodges will fall. I have watched and I have taken record. Many lodges will fall."

* * * * * * *

"Belmopan, I take access to Belmopan, it is Mine," says the Lord, "it is Mine."

* * * * * * *

"Jamaica will receive My justice, yes, Jamaica will receive My justice."

* * * * * * *

"In many nations they shake hands and scratch each others back but now My hand is taking control, son."

Tuesday 22nd March 2011.
I am looking down at Martinique and the island is in a frying pan being fried. There is a cord with one end attached to Martinique and the other end to France.

"Things are about to heat up, things are about to heat up greatly."

I see a scissors cut the cord and the fire under the frying pan dies. "I will bring peace, have no fear, I will bring peace."

Monday 4th April 2011.
"Jamaica is about to be turned upside down son. My will, will be done."

* * * * * * *

"Eritrea shall receive My shaking son. I shall dissolve their government, give them a new constitution and a new way of life."

* * * * * * *

"O Ethiopia, O Ethiopia I am coming in." I see Ethiopia lift off of the continent and travel high into the atmosphere with a great hand holding up the nation.

"You are the one I have chosen Ethiopia to be an example for Me on that continent. Great things are coming, great things are coming. I will also avenge what was done to you by the colonial, I will avenge. You and I have an agreement. It was signed many years ago. I have not forgotten you."

Tuesday 5th April 2011.
In RUSSIA, I see the land bulge upwards then cracks and a volcano rises from under the land. It erupts but the fire and lava are going upwards and it creates an orange looking atmosphere over the land.

"O yes they will be shaken son. They will be shaken."

Sunday 10th April 2011.
I see a golden lion with a crown on its head and fire in its eyes and it is running through out Ethiopia and each time it roars dark things like shadows leave the land.

* * * * * * *

"Abundance is coming Ecuador, abundance is coming."

* * * * * * *

Belmopan, I see a man at a river with a wooden box. At the bottom of the box is a wire mesh which looks as if it is used for sifting the river sand.
He has some sand in the box and shakes it in the river water but only pebbles with three gold nuggets are left and he says: "I have found nothing what will my people get."

"I have greater things for them. I will establish greater things for them. I set up greater things for them, for the old things will be removed. The old tools and ways of looking for wealth will be changed. They will have access in My new ways."

Sunday 1st May 2011.
"Jamaica shall be hidden for a time. For a season I will cover them and then all of a sudden they shall burst out into glory and greater things like never before. Greater things shall be seen."

* * * * * * *

Italy, I see a man like a butcher with his apron on and the butcher's knife is in his hand. He cuts Italy in half and pushes the southern part away into the Mediterranean Sea.

"Now it's My turn, for I will rule this land and bring all things to alignment."

* * * * * * *

"Vancouver, British Columbia. Get it right, get it right. Its time for them to get it right. I am coming in."

I see angels passing over Vancouver and saying: "Get it right and prepare a place for Me I am coming in."

"British Columbia will explode in My glory all they have to do is get it right."

* * * * * * *

I see a white sheet pulled over Milwaukee, Wisconsin. "Not to fear, not to fear I have you covered. The prayers of the saints, I heard the prayers of the saints, I have you covered."

* * * * * * *

Jamaica, I see Jamaica shaking in the sea. "A shaking is coming but I will exercise restraint. But you will be shaken."

* * * * * * *

"Mozambique, you keep testing Me, you keep testing Me. You know what you have to do, when will you totally trust Me."

* * * * * * *

Botswana, I see a cover removed and snakes fighting with each other. One snake in the east and the other in the west and they are snapping and fighting but the one from the west swallows the one from the east then the western snake dies.

"It is over says God, it is over. They tried to rule over Me but they devoured each other, it is over."

* * * * * * *

"Mozambique, the sea will come against them, it will come against them." I see a huge wave come in and cover Mozambique.

* * * * * * *

"British Columbia will maneuver towards Me."

Monday 9th May 2011.
"Guatemala, I will make them spicy to the taste, nourishing with much to give as I invest much. I will channel things differently. A new way of operations, a new way of standards. This land I am taking the dark cover from over them."

I see a great hand pull a sheet of darkness off of Guatemala.

"Many lies have been told but I will clean it up and you will hear about it in the media. I see a white rock coming down from the sky and hitting Guatemala as if it was a nuclear bomb but no devastation just a cleansing that goes through out the land and everything looks crystal white."

Tuesday 10th May 2011.
"Nicaragua, you will know that I am real and My hand is for you, but be warned for past things still haunt you and you dwell on the bloodshed. But know that I am cleaning your land so I can come in at a greater measure. Nothing shall stop Me, and nothing shall stop the work I shall do for this land by My power."

I see fireworks launched out of Nicaragua that create a mushroom affect in the sky.

* * * * * * *

"Belmopan, O Belmopan. As you sift for gold I will sift you. As you sift for gold I will build you. As you sift for gold I will make you. O Belmopan I have great plans. Greater things are coming."

I see ships coming and taking gold but I hear voices saying: "Pay us what is due to us. It is ours, it is ours." I see money by the handful going into the country.

* * * * * * *

"Egypt, it has just begun. Greater things are coming. My plans will be established, My will, will be done."

* * * * * * *

"Son, I am about to visit the old and ancient nations that are still functioning. They received My gospel but forgot Me. From Rome, to the north, from Jerusalem, to the south even Babylon and Persia, even the far east. O yes the early Church was fearless but I am about to visit those nations again."

* * * * * * *

Belgium, I see a pancake being cooked and as it is flipped one side is well cooked and is dark brown and the other side is cream colored as if it is not well cooked.

"Both sides will glorify Me. How it looks is how I want it son. Both sides will glorify Me."

* * * * * * *

"St Kitts, Martinique and the other islands. I cleave you, I cleave you." I see a great hand scoop up the islands of the West Indies and squeeze them together and when the hand is open I see a solid gold rock. "O yes, O yes it is going to be done."

* * * * * * *

"Paris, France will be split in half." I see an axe come down and split the Eiffel Tower in half right down to the foundation. But it joins back together and it looks tired as if it wants to faint. Eventually it falls as a man would faint. It then stands up again.

"I give you life, life, life, life."

* * * * * * *

"Martinique, you are the jewel that will cause others to be bold. You are the jewel that will cause others to be forthright; you are the jewel that will cause others to be unmovable. Martinique, the example for the freedom of others."

Tuesday 17th May 2011.
I see a giant metal bucket over Belize and it is pouring sand on Belize. The sand looks white in color. In the sand are green crystals that look like emeralds as well as white diamonds and gold nuggets.

When the bucket is empty it is turned to face heaven and it gets full again then pours on Belize and so it happens over and over again. Each time the bucket faces heaven to be filled I hear: "Season come, season go."

I noticed a giant man in the atmosphere over Belize and He is holding the bucket. He has on a long white robe and I cannot see His feet but He has a smile on His face.

"I make you strong Belize, I make you rich. Take care of your own, Protect what I give you and I say protect."

* * * * * * *

Tuesday 24th May 2011.
"Martinique will receive My fire and they are going to be strong enough to pull away."

Wednesday 8th June 2011.
"I hold Israel in My fist," says the Lord, "and their enemies will not prevail."

* * * * * * *

"Martinique shall not be moved. What I have planed for them will come to pass."

* * * * * * *

"Grace, grace, grace I give to the ancient places in the far east, grace."

* * * * * * *

Nairobi Kenya, I see big and tall buildings coming out of the soil and touching the sky. "I am bringing them up higher."

Saturday 11th June 2011.

"Their enemies will stand at their gates but not subdue them. Israel is strong as My arm is strong and will not degenerate but great increase as I move among them, because I have not forgotten My promises and what I originally said about this land.

O Israel hear My voice I am still with you and I will not be moved. Your borders are strong as I am strong, your might cannot be over run as I cannot be over run so fear no man and no nation.

You have erred in decision making because of outside interference but I am still strong and you are strong.

Your enemies will not have you, they will never have you. You are Mine Israel and who can take you out of My hand. You have been fed from My mouth, I nourished you and you are strong.

Lift up your eyes O nation, unplug your ears and hear Me, hear Me. I still speak as I did in the old days, in the days of your ancient fathers I still speak. So listen and you will hear Me again. When the beast comes against you do not be afraid of his words because they are empty as a barking dog on a short leash who cannot do any harm.

O Israel, O Israel My hand is for you as I brushed aside your enemies in the desert. So I will do again, and again, and again. None will stand against you and prosper. You are still My child. I am still your inheritance. Come to Me child, come to Me, come to Me again."

I see black dogs coming out of the desert and racing towards Israel from all sides but they are stopped at the borders and cannot enter.

"They cannot crossover," says God. "They will never crossover. I have created barriers, fixed things in place that will not be moved."

I see ghost ships, old and derelict with holes in them and old sails with holes in it. Those ships are coming towards Israel on the Mediterranean Sea, but they sink before reaching the shores of Israel and they lie at the bottom of the sea.

"Those ships were bringing death to Israel. Sickness and diseases, famine and drought. Even insects with death in them. They would have devoured crops, total desolation.

But I moved," said God, "and I will continue to move for the protection of My child. Hear the word of the Lord Israel; hear the word of the Lord. Look to Me again I am still for you."

Wednesday 15th June 2011.
"I am about to put My foot down in many nations son. For many nations are about to feel a heaviness because I am about to humble them. They ask if I am real, they question if I am alive but I am about to prove Myself in ways that they cannot deny that I am God. Their false gods will crumble. They will see the wood and the stone that is dead. They will know that I rule and I reign and I direct.

Even the seas I will move in some strange ways and even science will be baffled and call it an occurrence but it is Me the All Mighty bringing man to acknowledge Me.

O the nations have blasphemed, O the nations have shown Me no respect but now it's My turn. I have looked, and looked and I have allowed but now it's My turn.

Their nice and wonderful things shall taste bitter. Their image shall be altered where one nation shall not be the star on the earth for even a nation can be seen as god. I am God.

I am removing the chains that man have put on some nations and those very chains I will put on those who enslave others. I am still a just God.

They look at the calamities on the earth and wonder if I am love. How can God do this to us, but they sin against Me, and sin against Me, and sin against Me. A father disciplines the child for wrong. Can I not do the same. I am the Father above all fathers and without Me their would be no fathers. Look and see son, look and see the famines, look and see the dry lands, look and see the sea come in and take away lives with it. Even your land is marked for a specific day, even your land will be judged. In your land are liars and wicked people stand on the pulpit. Wicked people give direction and in your law offices the enemy rules but it's about My name and I will drive out who have to be driven out, I will break the backs. The government deals will go down instead of up. Those who have compromised will be thrown out and you wonder why. You have tied your hands with stone and wood and expect Me to stand with you. Did you stand with Me. My name, My name is on this land and it shall not be moved."

"Other nations gather together seeking solutions, seeking partnerships but they don't seek Me. So what solutions, and what partnerships, and what peace because without Me the barrels will be empty waiting for substance to full it but no substance will come. Without Me no substance."

I see a clock on a wall, ticking.

"See the clock son, see the time ticking away. I am the time and I have given much grace but they have abused My grace and taken Me for granted; so My sword shall come in many ways and I will prove to them that their gods are no god at all."

I see an ancient sword washed up on the shores of India then it sinks into the soil and the earth retaliates by shaking and cracking. Smoke comes out of the cracks and the earth is moved up and down.

Note: The ancient sword I saw was curved and looked similar to a sickle. In India it is called a "Kirpans."

"Many nations will discover that I am real and I speak and I have been watching. If the nations repent I will hold back My hand but they won't son they won't. A hard people is on the earth, a rebellious people is on the earth and My house is no better and I hold My house responsible for many things.
For liars and deceivers carry My word and mingle it with their purpose, their own wants and desires. Many are deceived because

they don't seek Me for themselves and deception rules but I am coming son, I am coming into My house as a man comes home after a long journey away and he comes and clean and put things in order. Don't worry son they have been warned, they have been cautioned so they have no excuse. I am coming to take back My house. Many will be driven away and young ones will lead the flock. I have shown you in My word about those who don't feed the flock but feed themselves. But I will raise up those who will feed My flock while I bring an end to greed.

See the television son, see the television, see the greed, see the show, see the image that detestable image they portray. It's coming to an end son, its coming to an end. Hear the radio do you hear the competition on the radio. I will kill the signal and the ears will be turned off then I will cause the ear to be turned on again to those who are true. They have made a mockery of Me and I will stand for it no longer.

What poor do they feed, what houses do they build. They fly around in their private planes but I fly higher, they drive around in their expensive cars but all the gold is Mine, they showoff their houses while My house is in shambles. The spiritual walls are broken down, the spiritual roofs have fallen and they boast in what I give them. Thieves son, thieves. Thieves and robbers whose heart is as dark as a dungeon but they proclaim light. They build but I never told them to build, they break down but I never told them to break down, they eat and get sick My temple is desecrated. Hidden things that are in the temple bring sickness. Many seek doctors before Me, many seek medical care before Me. I tell you son they have put Me on the back seat.

Must I be treated as a little slave boy, must I be treated with scorn. I tell you son their hearts are not after Me so My heart is not with them. Sickness rules the temple. Before their time many will fall and go away, before their time. But those who are true to Me I will raise up and give them a sure footing and a great voice.

Don't worry about what religion has done to My house that's why I have you. You have not seen the full purpose of why I have you. They don't know who you are but suddenly and shocking they will find out. O the nations of the earth. I am calling them as the hen calls her chicks. Speak My word and fear no man. I have spoken son and all things will come to pass. I will prove you and I will prove who I say you are.

They say you are a madman but they do the same things over and over again expecting Me to show up in new ways so who is the madman. The prophets with the sweet words I am bringing them down. Even in your land I have brought one to his knees and others will follow. The liars are coming down son, the liars are coming down.

Soon I will tell you what is happening in the bible schools. Write every word and leave nothing out."

Thursday 16th June 2011.
"I have seen what they have done to My house. Changes are coming and some will have to step down because they refuse to change.

Changes are coming because it is My house and man have made it his ministry and his calling but without Me they have nothing. See the lies, see their way, see the tricks like an illusionist. They are full of tricks and they have a good audience, an audience that don't know Me but I am coming in. I am coming in hard and who have to be plucked out will be without remedy. Much lies and much tricks are being done.

On the workplace they have sold Me out. The men have become slaves and the women are prostitutes. They will not stand and they will not let righteousness reign. They have sold out son; they have sold out on the workplaces. Many of them worship their job and the bank account is their supreme god but My people are rotting on the inside, rotting, rotting, rotting and the false joy and happiness of the world have them captive.

Do you think I want you to be part of this? Never! Watch them son, watch them because they are a people that refuse to change and they will try and change you and put laws on you because of their status and image.

The image rules My house, the image infatuated My house, its all about image. Do you think I want you to be part of that.

Many of them don't know who they are so they copy another, they drink the spirit of another. Possessed by the spirit of another man and controlled by the puppeteer.

O son I am about to do great things with you, great, great things and… They don't know who you are."

* * * * * * *

"Martinique, I send a call to Martinique, the process have begun. I will cause your own hand to work for you Martinique."

* * * * * * *

"Barbados, you colonial place. The land clenched with a colonial fist. I release you and your pride will fall but not all is gone. But I must deal with your pride.

O how proud you are of your colonial history and your present links to the old master. Am I not "The Master," The Master of righteousness and truth, the Master who gives true freedom and I say to you again true freedom. You hold on to that pride but it will be broken, o yes it will. I AM GOD."

* * * * * * *

Guadeloupe, I see in the sea to the east of you a whirlpool. It's not pulling anything in but its sending three things out. Three ribbons: black, red and blue ribbons. Each ribbon lay across your land east to west. Under each ribbon trees are rising up strong and flourishing, mountains are rising lush and green, the city is being built with strong tall buildings.

"I have plans says God, I have plans."

Friday 17th June 2011.

"I walk among the nations, I move among the nations and they don't recognize Me. So I shake their land, I shake their homes, I shake their governments. The earth is Mine and I will shake it.

Many systems grieve Me because it only benefits one group of people while many suffer, so it will crumble. I will take it apart like a puzzle and they will not find the pieces. Suddenly those with power will find their hands empty, the pen will not have the ink to sign the documents that give away what belongs to others. Suddenly their wallets are empty and their houses are fallen.

Some houses of old where darkness lives and some new houses. They will fall. Surely son they will fall.

I am rooting up in education. Some great houses of education where they plot and plan I am rooting up. Much evil has been passed on and the things that do not acknowledge Me I will root up. I sweep away lies, I sweep away lies.

I cause you to see between the lines and see the lies. Get ready son get ready.

This is the place, the place of education where lies are passed on. This is the place where the Church have allowed My name to be blasphemed. This is the place where the enemy stands and exalts himself. There are those who have drank from his cup, that is no good to My Church. But soon a storm is moving across the earth that will root up deep rooted stony things that would not shake. Now it will be plucked up like a weed and truth will take its place."

"They say they are schools of the bible but they compromise for funding. They say they are schools of the bible but they compromise for approval. They say they are schools of the bible but they compromise for notoriety. Much more I will tell you, because many schools carry My name but My Spirit is not their. I left them and in many cases I was never their.

Do you know the enemy started some bible schools with the strategy to poison the Church? Many leaders who say they are under Me do not know Me. They know of Me but they don't know Me.

You know anyone can achieve the certificate, you know anyone can get the degree but how many are with Me?

Many speak to Me but don't know My voice. Many teach My word but don't know My word they know a system, a system of how to do it. If I was to visit some they won't believe it is Me because their system have no room for Me.

It's all about man, son, its all about man. Yes, in the bible schools they worship man. Most students don't even have My heart. Another step up the ladder but where is My heart."

I see students in a bible school and I see their hearts beating. The hearts are red in color. They are beating for each other, beating for the lecturer and beating for self.

"They choose leaders by charisma, they choose leaders by education, they choose leaders by name but many leaders don't know My name. For many of them it's just another job and it's not because they love Me. But I am coming in, know for sure son, I am coming in. Even if they pray to choose a leader many of them made a choice before praying. Praying became a formality the choice was made before.

Favoritism, I am going to break the back of favoritism that ugly thing will not run My house. That ugly thing will not mock Me. My chosen have been tossed aside, My chosen have been put on the back seat I am coming in, son, I am coming in."

I see a bright light in the form of a man tossing things aside in a classroom and He is in a rage.

"Many bible schools have no justice. Many bible schools have no truth. Many bible schools have become a house of whores. They sell their gifting for something in return. They sell themselves for something in return. They are raising up whores. They are doing it son, they are doing it. And they are using My name. I am coming in, I am coming in.

Move out of My way you detestable thing. Move out of My way you ugly thing. Move out of My way you faction of whores. I see you, I see you all, I see your heart beat and it is not with Me. That ladder you are climbing will break. That stair you are moving up will crumble and you will loose your footing and fall right back down. It is now My turn," says God, "it is now My turn. The mockery is over.

Much lies, much lies are spoken in secret places. Secret places of the mind and secret places of their spirit. They plot and plan how to win friends for an open door. Now do you understand son, now do you see how they do it. It's just another business deal. You will not follow such things and I have already put it in you to resists such things. The ugliness, the tremendous ugliness.

At times you will feel as if you are out in the cold but that doesn't mean they are secure in Me. Do not be deceived by how things look. They seal the deal just like the world. They shake hands with the spirit of the world. Do not be part of it. O yes, they will throw stones. Do not be part of it.

It's no longer about brother loving brother and sister loving sister, but it's about what can I get from that person and what can that person do for Me. They have raised up whores son, whores. Its ugly and the stench sickens Me.

I refuse the prayers of whores, I block My ears when the prayers of whores come up to Me, I refuse.

Transparency, what transparency lies and deception hidden in their secret places. I told you I am changing the guard but I will speed it up, enough."

* * * * * * *

"There are those who know you are not cursed. There are those I spoke to but they were afraid to talk because they would have been rebuked. I spoke to them and told them the truth."

* * * * * * *

"You are not poor, and I am taking care of you."

Saturday 18th June 2011.
"The lying prophets are coming down. I have watched and I have listened. Those whose souls are as black as midnight where deception and manipulation rules and My Spirit have been given no respect, they are coming down.

Some started off right, but O the dollar. The dollar became their mother and the approval of man became their father and their heart is no longer Mine.

You sweetheart prophets your words run like honey. Evil men stood before you and you gave them a spoon of honey instead of My wrath that brings them to repentance. Wicked women with no shame came to you and you had a smile, flirting in your heart.

But now it is finished, I am crushing your mother and your father. You have made yourselves gods in the eyes of man but now man will see what you are really made of. Repent, repent I am coming after you and I have no mercy."

* * * * * * *

"I have placed watchmen over every nation and they will report to you son, from time to time they will report to you."

Daniel 4:13. I saw in the visions of my head while on my bed, and there was <u>a watcher</u>, a holy one, coming down from heaven. NKJV.

Daniel 4:17. This decision is by the decree of <u>the watchers</u>, and the sentence by the word on the holy ones, in order that the living may know that the Most High rules in the kingdom of men… NKJV.

The NIV version says "messengers" instead of "watchers."

Monday 4th July 2011.
I see an arrow on fire coming out of the sky, from between the clouds and it is heading for Jerusalem.

"I am coming. Israel I am coming with My fire and I will not miss the mark, I never do. I am on My way towards you and a great fire will start. I come to consume and I come to set ablaze, I come to burn down and I come to purify, I come to chase away and I come to expose.

My fire is on its way and I have My targets the homes to be restored. The overthrowing of wrong to introduce light. Here I come and I have My targets in sight. Do not turn from Me this is for your benefit. Do not reject Me I come to set things right."

I see tears falling off the face of Jesus and falling on Jerusalem.

"I have wept over you but one day soon I will have tears of joy because of you. O Israel we will rejoice together. I have watched Jerusalem, I see all things and I am sending My fire."

Saturday 9th July 2011.
"What Christian business, do they love their employees? What Christian business, do they give out of love or to get something in return?

They boast of their giving and come to Me for something in return. Am I their lackey? Am I their boy?

Their hands are crafty just as the other man, their ways are deceiving just as the other man, and some of them wear many different masks."

I see an old man skinny and dry to the bone and he is in a house that is dimly lit. He is standing in front of a table with an old fashioned scale on it and he is trying to make the scale balanced but it is not balancing.

"O how dry they are son, dry to the bone and deceiving prophets have gone to them and the sweet words beguiled them. Their scales will never balance because their heart and motive is not with Me. If I were to take away their possessions many of them would not stay with Me.

The reason why the room is dim lit is because My presence which is light is gone. Many of them belong to the brotherhood of darkness and put on a nice parade on Sunday morning but I see their heart that is not with Me.

I am removing their cover and the authorities will move against them and many of their business doors will close.

Son, they lie and steal and trick just as the other man.

Son, their hearts are not with Me. Their hearts cannot be found.

Is their seed sowing out of love? Some come to My face and make demands but I am about to humble many and many will be humiliated. I will tell you whose business to bless and whose business not to bless because some of them are bold in their tricks, son. Bold with their tricks.

Do you remember these words, "I can't help you unless you work for me." That so called Christian employer would have enslaved you. I bring to remembrance these words, "I won't come down on you and run you off, I will keep you here and fight you." Just because you disagreed with him and didn't flow his way. See the spirit son, see how they operate. And they use My word in their filth, they use My word in their wickedness. I want you to see son, I want you to learn."

I see many houses of business on the earth and they are all dimly lit and blend in with the dark atmosphere on the outside. I see the houses being pulled up and thrown off the planet then new houses rise on the earth with red roofs and white walls but on the inside is a great glow that cannot be contained so it radiates on the outside and illuminates the atmosphere.

"O, what I am about to do. For I will inspire others those who don't believe they could have had a business. I will make others pregnant and their hearts will be right and ripe."

"Much wrong has been done to you, much wrong and I am taking record."

* * * * * * *

"Many of them who talk about integrity only have it in certain areas of life, especially to impress but I see their hearts. No integrity in the hearts. I see the operations of their hearts, I hear the thoughts. No integrity son and I am not moved, I have yet to be touched. Many right things are done but the motives have nothing to do with Me. They impress, son they impress and I am not moved."

Tuesday 19th July 2011.
"Taiwan, I shall spank you," says God. "I shall spank you as a child. I see your mischief; I see your hidden things the crafty ways a child deceives. You are still young Taiwan. Your feet are not strong; your muscles have not come to maturity."

I see fireworks, bright lights and celebration.

"You like the fireworks and the spectacle but I will soon shake you. Not all will be lost but you will recognize Me. I am true Taiwan, I am real and I am a better dancer than the dragon."

* * * * * * *

"Mozambique, hurry up and get it done."

I see empty coconut shells about a dozen and they all look the same but under one of them is what looks like a marble. The shells are moved around but no one tries to find the one with the marble.

"I give you access and you are not trying Mozambique. Reach out and see what I will do. I will put the right one in place at the right time. You have My favor."

Sunday 7th August 2011.
I saw a great fist smash into Mt Rushmore and all the presidential faces crumbled and fell.

"I am coming against their pride. They must know that I am coming against their pride."

Monday 8th August 2011.
Concerning the word from God about watchmen over every nation and then reporting to me. I decided to walk into it.

"Listen carefully son for you are about to walk in another aspect. Each watchman carries the same name of the nation he is watching. I know you are about to call them and they will report but be sharp to listen and quick in understanding. The place I have put you in guard it carefully. For wicked men are on the earth and wicked people are in My house."

"Watchman of Germany, I call you."

"The people of Germany they are working and they will boom and I will strengthen their hand. Some of them are still carrying the heaviness of past history but I will remove that burden and they will hold their head up. There are those who trace their history to those who followed Hitler and shame follows them but God will move and that generational shame will be removed but some are proud so they will be broken."

I see the Spirit stretching Germany so it overlaps the surrounding nations.

"This is for good because Germany will cause the nations around them to be secure."

The watchman of Germany then departed.

* * * * * * *

"Watchman of Israel, I call you."

I see the Spirit in the clouds over Israel dancing and singing to God.

"I have been waiting for you. I have been expecting you to call Me. Now know that soon they will be dancing and singing again. I will fall on them and they will rejoice. This is warfare, this is warfare man of God. Dancing and singing is war."

He then returned to His place over Israel.

* * * * * * *

"Watchman of France, I call you."

A man in a military uniform came to me. He saluted and made his report.

"Our arms will be stretched throughout the earth but it will be for a good and we will help other nations maintain their peace."

He then made an about turn and departed.

* * * * * * *

Sunday 14th August 2011.
Puerto Rico, I see an arrow enter your land. It enters from the east and the tip of it exits facing west. It is stuck in Puerto Rico.

"I shoot straight says God. I will strike the heart of the land at the heart of every issue. Not a wound to kill but every issue will be struck on target."

* * * * * * *

"Belmopan, mistakes of the past I throw it away. Belmopan, bad decisions I toss behind you. My sun is shining on you and My hand is for you."

Monday 15th August 2011.
"Watchman of Dominica, I call you."

A brown skinned man came to me with a basket of bananas. Some of the bananas are ripe and ready, some are rotten and some have worms. The worms are consuming the bananas.

"They need help, their crops are infested and they need help but soon I will send rain and wash away the infestation and a cleansing. Their products will be top grade, highly sought after and this infestation will be eradicated. I am cleansing them and I am cleansing their land and I am cleansing their products.
Man of God, know that there is much wickedness on the earth and there are assignments to keep certain nations poor and dependant but I am God and it will be broken."

Friday 26th August 2011.
Barbados, I see a palm tree rise out of the land. It is tall and strong reaching to the clouds. The branches shade the island from the blistering sun but then a storm comes and the palm tree sways violently in the wind until it brakes near the base and fall into the sea. Then rough storm waters flood over Barbados.

"I kept them for many years but now I am stirring up the elements against them."

Wednesday 31st August 2011.
For the past two days I have been seeing a cauldron in the atmosphere over Trinidad. The cauldron has a fire beneath it and it is filled with boiling water. The cauldron then tilts and the boiling water is poured out on Trinidad.

"They went too far, there is going to be a boiling over, things will heat up. When people are restricted they will eventually lash out. They went too far. They are abusing their powers. Race is behind it son, race is behind it. Its boiling, it's boiling."

Thursday 8<u>th</u> September 2011.
"Pakistan, mayhem is about to happen in Pakistan, great mayhem."

* * * * * * *

Indonesia, I see a hand gently moving back the waters and under the water and in the sand I see what looks like emeralds. The hand lifts the green emeralds up to me and said:

"See what they have."

* * * * * * *

Pakistan, I see a Chinese Terracotta warier and it is held by a hand that is pounding the land of Pakistan. The terracotta warier crumbles, the hand turns to clay and it also crumbles.

"Mysteries, mysteries, mysteries. Ancient mysteries for this land."

* * * * * * *

"Indonesia. So rich, so rich, O so rich."

Monday 12<u>th</u> September 2011.
I see a giant broom sweeping the desert surface of Libya and as it sweeps it uncovers an iron surface that looks as if it is the top of an underground bunker or hiding place.

"Secret things are about to be exposed, secret hidden things."

* * * * * * *

I see a cooking pot out in the Egyptian desert. People from all directions are coming to drink from the pot and are running back to where they came from. But giant waves of water are coming against them and they are vomiting because of what they drank from the pot in the desert.

****

The Seychelles Islands; I see a whirlpool suck them in and spit them out, but this time they look like nuggets of gold in the sea.

****

Mauritania: I see a hand tapping the land and pushing you to the west.

Sunday 18th September 2011.
"Trinidad and Tobago. St Joseph, the first things planted, the first things established I will cause My Church to come against you. A rooting up. Deep, deep roots are coming up and many things will be driven out. A refreshing and a new land. I will send a refreshing. There is a stronghold in St Joseph a religious domain where pride stands firm. Look at the old Churches and even the cemetery and you will see pride. Even your police and other services operate with that spirit. O what was planted.
Son, they did things to claim the land, they planted things in the ground to claim this land so they can control, maneuver and get the people where they want them.
They did not only establish a capitol but they also establish a hold."

I see a man in an old colonial European military uniform with his right hand on the ground and he is claiming the land but he is doing it in the name of the religious church. Behind the military officer is standing a priest dressed in his robe and head piece with a rod and at the top of the rod is a silver crucifix.

"They have done this to many nations son, and those nations are struggling to be free."

Tuesday 27th September 2011.
God gave me this scripture for the nations.

James 5:1-3. Come now, you rich, weep and howl for your miseries that are coming upon you. Your riches are corrupted and your garments are moth eaten. Your gold and silver are corroded and their corrosion will be a witness against you and will eat your flesh like fire. You have heaped up treasure in the last days. Nkjv.

* * * * * * *

God gave me this scripture for His Church.

Jeremiah 9:19. For a voice of wailing is heard from Zion: How we are plundered. We are greatly ashamed. Because we have forsaken the land because we have been cast out of our dwellings. Nkjv.

Thursday 29th September 2011.
I saw a rich green vine but still young and it came out of the land in Mexico. It wrapped around and squeezed Mexico until milk and liquid came out of the land.

"Soon someone will rise son, young with much potential. At first look the people will love him but then the true man will be seen."

I see on the inside of the vine there is a heart and it is black and shriveled up. One of the branches of the vine is holding a book and on the book is written the word "law". The book is placed on a table and the vine moves on then a dark thing as a shadow passes over the book and it turns to ashes.

"Disturbance is coming son, disturbance is coming. In high levels disturbance is coming."

Thursday 6th October 2011.
In Romania I see a statue of a man painted in white and he is on a white pedestal. A hand comes and take the statue off of the pedestal and hits it on the ground and the head of the statue brakes off then the statue is returned to the pedestal.

"They will know that I rule and I am the head. They will turn son they will turn."

Sunday 9th October 2011.
I see a great hand over Belgium and in the palm of the hand is a green leaf. The hand releases the leaf and it slowly and gently comes down on the land of Belgium. As the leaf rests on the land it moves snow and cold weather and everything starts looking lush and green with the homes and buildings now lit up where it used to be dark.

"I will visit them, I hold in My hands what they need but I will visit them."

* * * * * * *

I see a bartender in Acapulco shaking mixed drinks with a smile on his face and with his other hand he is using his finger to call people towards him. His face then becomes sad and he puts down the drink and he says: "our luster is gone our pride is fallen."

"You have made many drunk with your spirit says God, you have enticed many with your ways. The false things about you are exposed and now it's My turn says God, now its My turn. I have taken away your pride."

* * * * * * *

In Venice I see a man in a small river boat transporting people but then the river dries up and the boat sits at the bead of the river and the man looks around in amazement and disbelief.

"O yes, you too Venice, you will loose your pride and you will know Me and My workings. You will know Me I guarantee it. My grace is coming, it is coming."

I see a hand pushing what looks like a mist or cloud on Venice and it is meant to bring peace.

* * * * * * *

"O Jerusalem, Jerusalem, Jerusalem My visitation is near, My empowering is near."

I still see the arrow on fire released from the bow and heading for Jerusalem.

* * * * * * *

I see the tall buildings in Chicago bowing to the west in submission and saying: "We worship You, O Lord, we submit to you our God. What we have done we submit, what we have done we repent. Remove the blood from our streets, remove the stain and the stigma."

I see a man with a gun in his hand. He puts the gun in his pocket and walk into Church. He is at the alter and he puts the gun down on the alter and has his hands up in surrender then great light hits him and he turns glowing white and leaves the Church dancing and singing.

* * * * * * *

I see New York sink into the sea and come up again.

"Again I wash you, again I give you another chance. Know Me before My judgment comes."

* * * * * * *

In Colorado I see geysers sprouting up all over the state.

"Un-expectantly I come without them knowing, I show up. I am greater then a mile, supreme above every mile. I sit in the heavens. I am the Most High and higher than a mile. Suddenly I come. I sprout and shoot and I come."

Friday 21st October 2011.
I saw the island of Tobago tumbling in the sea. It then tumbled towards Trinidad and then returned to its original geographic position.

"Your little sister have played the harlot but I will soon restore her dignity."

Saturday 22nd October 2011.
Ecuador, I see a white rose blooming and from the midst of the rose it spits blood and the whole rose turns red.

"I will cleanse them again, o yes I will cleanse them again."

* * * * * * *

I saw a Bengal Tiger standing on the map of India. It growled at me then its face turned sad and it collapsed or fainted. I reached down and laid my hands on it and it sprang back to life. Then it said: "thank you, from all of us. Thank you."

* * * * * * *

"Ethiopia shall prevail, in war Ethiopia shall prevail."

Saturday 12th November 2011.
"Toronto will explode with glory. I will cause Toronto to feel the effects of a spiritual volcano. My glory is coming, its on its way. look out Toronto."

Sunday 20th November 2011.
I see a rock on fire coming from the sky. The rock looks as if it is crystal and it lands in Haiti with such an affect that it creates a great crater and the whole land shakes. The whole land turns crystal as the rock. On the surface the whole nation is crystal but on the bottom it looks red in color.

"God is coming Haiti, God is coming."

Monday 28th November 2011.
I see blood tipped swords hanging in the atmosphere above Africa. The swords fall and pierce those men who wear the crowns and they are in agony. As the men are pierced, money falls out of one hand and out of the other hand falls gold and diamonds. Out of their mouth flows oil and oil also comes out of the wound caused by the sword.

"Those who have sold out their own, their time is over. Look and see son, look and see the fall of great men. I have just begun, their time is over."

I see a giant angel standing in Africa. He is half white and half black from head to feet. He looked at me and said "You look." In his right hand is a sword drenched in blood and in his left hand is an old fashioned scale.
As he steps on one nation he looks at the scale and if it is balanced he moves on but if it is off balanced he slaughters. And he moves from nation to nation in Africa.

Sunday 1st January 2012.
I am looking at the nations from Mexico down to Panama and I see light coming out of those nations. Then what looks like young plants are coming out of the soil and rising up.

"One day, one time, one season they will flourish."

Tuesday 10th January 2012.
I saw Martinique lift out of the sea and travel high into the atmosphere.

"Greater things are coming for them. Beyond their expectations."

Saturday 4th February 2012.
I see a chimney and white smoke coming out of it. Then I see red smoke and black smoke and they all blend.

"Trinidad and Tobago, things are heating up beneath the smoke. Your politicians are blowing smoke but things are heating up, rapidly heating up. Be warned great fire is coming they are fanning the flames. A great fire."

Monday 6th February 2012.
"Leningrad, you once were. You once had power, you once had authority. But I swiftly changed you, but your spirit still has influence. You still sway in making decisions so I am coming in deeper and even the mind will be changed. I revolutionize the mind and cause them to see beyond the old status."

I see a lush green tree which deteriorates turning brown as it dwindles. All the leaves fall off and the tree looks like a weathered skeleton.
I see years rapidly going by and a man with an axe chops down the tree and only the stomp is left. The stomp tries to spring back to life but a dark thing as a shadow comes on it and it eventually dies down to the rotting of the roots.

"You will not return and give influence, you will not return and give influence, you will not return and give influence."

* * * * * * *

"Ipswich, I know your cause." I see a tunnel beneath a street and a man is calling others and leading them through the tunnel. As they pass the tunnel collapses behind them and even the street caves in and cars on the street fall in.

"Many made it through but the time has come to an end."

* * * * * * *

"London Bridge is falling down, falling down, falling down. London Bridge is falling down, falling down, falling down."

"History is about to change. I turn the page, I make a new way. The old guard is gone, I put a new man."

* * * * * * *

Helsinki, I see a white flag flying at half mast and a soldier in his uniform is looking up at it and saying "when are they going to put the thing back up don't they know it's over. We have grieved enough, the people have grieved enough."

I see a light gray cloud over the land and it is causing heaviness over the land and on the people. A hand removes it and the people starts rejoicing as a dark thing come off of them.

* * * * * * *

"Jamaica, My word will be fulfilled, My will, will be done. Make no mistake it will all happen and all things will be brought near."

* * * * * * *

"Africa, make way for My Spirit it is coming." I see the Spirit of God come down from the sky and land in the heart of Africa and He is burning through the continent.

* * * * * * *

I see India lift out of its geographical place, spin three times and a hand is holding it up in the atmosphere.

"See what I can do, I will lift and exalt as I choose."

* * * * * * *

I see a Chinese man dancing in the streets of China but it is a strange dance as he grits his teeth and shakes his body.

"Strange things to identify that I am in the midst."

* * * * * * *

"Portugal, you will lift up a praise for Me, you will exalt My name. Don't you doubt. I will orchestrate everything and you will exalt Me."

* * * * * * *

"Rome has missed the mark again. They portray an image but they have missed the mark again."

* * * * * * *

"Rejoice O barren lands because I am coming to sustain you. I will refresh and make you wealthy. I make your people and generations strong. Your deserts will receive rain and your seas will be teaming with life. I make old things new and dead things life. The wombs will be fruitful with vibrant and strong children. Rejoice, rejoice I am coming."

* * * * * * *

Grenada, I see a hand lift you sideways and a Man is looking under you. Black snakes come out from the dark parts of your soil as they are exposed. The Man grabs the snakes and pulls them out and puts the top of Grenada back down.

"I remove the cover and the wickedness will be removed."

* * * * * * *

"Justice, justice My justice will prevail."

Saturday 25th February 2012.
"Watchman of Nigeria, I call you."

I see a man on his knees with his head bent. His hands are tied in front of him and his feet are tied beneath him.
Another man with a cutlass is standing at his side and he lifts the cutlass and chops off the head of the man who is kneeling.

"They are turning on their own, internal destruction. The land will be weakened."

I see a great deal of people running and the man with the cutlass chasing them and as he catches up with them he is chopping at will.

"Mayhem, it is started. Mayhem, it is started. Another land to be divided."

* * * * * * *

"Watchman of Ireland, I call you."

I see a man in the clouds over Ireland and he is dressed in the Irish national dress. He has a club in his hand and it looks as if he is fighting the wind.

"They are wasting time on things that don't add up but solution is coming. I will give them the solution, I will give them the answer."

* * * * * * *

"Watchman of Germany, I call you."

"Must we please the world? We don't have to please the world. I was put here to take care of these people. They don't have to please the world."

* * * * * * *

"Watchman of France, I call you."

I see a man in an old world war one plane. He has a mustache with a scarf around his neck and goggles on his eyes. He is circling the Eiffel Tower and the tower has a red flashing light on the top.

"Much of the old ways I will take it away."

* * * * * * *

"Watchman of Belgium, I call you."

I see a woman in their national dress with what looks like a pouch at her side. Her hair is blond and combed in two long plats.
She is just beneath the clouds and dancing in a straight line while she dips her hand in the pouch and brings out corn. The corn seeds are put in a circle over Belgium then she says "fall" and the seeds fall on the land and the corn trees grow much larger than normal.

"Quick sustenance, I provide much for them."

* * * * * * *

"Watchman of Yugoslavia, I call you."

I see a man in brown winter coat and he is digging at the side of a mountain. He finds something wrapped in cloth that looks like a small bowling pin.

He lifts it up to the sky and shouts "This is all you can give us?" A giant statue of a man with a folk in his right hand comes down and land on the mountain top. He is made of stone but he crumbles and falls apart.

"Their old things will be no more. I will show them where to find the greater. I will come down and show them."

* * * * * * *

"Watchman of Greece, I call you."

I see a man in the clouds above Greece and he is walking bent over as if he is tired and has no more strength. But then great light from above hits him and a darkness leaves him and he grows in strength and stature as his muscles grow bigger.
He then takes a lightening rod and sends it down to the land and as it lands it has a similar effect of an atomic bomb and everything radiates. The people look crystal white with their hands up and they are looking up towards the sky.

"When My strength is returned they will flourish."

Wednesday 7th March 2012.
"Watchman of Trinidad, I call you."

I see a man in the atmosphere dressed in black pants with a red and white frilled shirt and he is playing a tenor pan. I see several guns pointed at him. Men with smiles on their faces start shooting at him and he falls on his back, but his chest is still moving because his heart is still beating.
He then jumps to his feet quickly and starts playing the pan with a greater joy.

"For a time and a season, collapse but then what a revival."

"I was put here to sustain. Yes man of God I was put here to sustain. All that is happening is just for a time."

Friday 30th March 2012.
Afghanistan. I see a torpedo hit a mountain range and the mountain range becomes flat.

"I make all things even. I give no one the advantage."

Sunday 8th April 2012.
I see a giant mouth over Haiti and the tongue is speaking things of blasphemy over the nation. I also see a gold sword cut the tongue out of the mouth and the mouth retreats and disappears.
A rain cloud comes over Haiti and rains on the nation washing away darkness. The entire nation turns white with under the surface of the nation looking crystal. I see a coconut tree standing tall in Haiti. A coconut falls from the tree and rolls down the hill. It opens up and pretty butterflies of different varieties come out of the coconut. They travel all over the land and beautiful songs are heard.

"Great things are going to happen to that nation. I am going to showoff My power, showoff My might, showoff My love."

Saturday 12th May 2012.
"Mozambique. The trials are over, the liberation have come."

* * * * * * *

"Ecuador, I loose the rope."

I see a rope released and it is frozen in the spirit doing nothing.

"Ecuador you are loosed, Ecuador you are free, Ecuador its time for Me. I am coming and I am coming strong. My might, My might will fall on you. I am coming strong."

* * * * * * *

"Brazil, O the wondrous things, O the treasures. But you are to help others. Reach out and help and I will continually sustain you. I will cause a rift in your land so you can divide right from wrong and your poor will have bread and your weak will be strong. O Brazil, My wonders, My wonders are flowing through you. In your land, in your soil, in your heart flowing through you. I shall make the dance sweeter and the music will connect to Africa and do great things for Me. I am raising you, I am raising you mightily."

* * * * * * *

"Johannesburg, I am not finished with you Johannesburg. The spotlight will be on you again. A shaking, a shaking, a shaking."

* * * * * * *

I see Russia folding. The north east part is folded until it reaches the south west corners and the north western part is folded until it reaches the south eastern parts. Much of Russia is covered.

"They think they can cover up but I AM GOD and I will expose. You will see and you will hear son, much exposure."

* * * * * * *

"Watchman of the United States I call you."

I see a man draped in the American flag and he is stumbling as he moves along. It seems as if his left side is weak so he is stumbling towards the left.

"O man of God you will see and you will know. Their demands, their own demands have weakened them. Their privileges have spoilt them. You will give a hand and you will be a voice."

Saturday 16th June 2012.
I see a rocket launched out of China and it comes up into space. The front of the rocket opens and another rocket comes out. Then from this rocket comes something that looks like a probe which travels deep into space.

"Son, China is sending probes deep into space to search and to find out, but I will greatly disappoint them. I rule the heavenlies, I rule the boundaries on space and I hold all mysteries. I will disappoint and I will permit, but I rule."

* * * * * * *

"China is lying about many things. China is lying about many things."

Monday 25th June 2012.
I saw the Island of Cyprus with a book on it. The book is opened and the pages are turning quickly but the pages are empty. As the turning pages come close to the end of the book it stops and there is a check mark on one of the pages.

"Later on I will approve them."

Sunday 1st July 2012.
"Watchman of Ireland I call you."

I see a man making a bed. It is a big bed with double mattresses and a wooden frame. At the four corners of the bed are wooden pillars.
The man is tucking in the sheets between the mattresses and says to me "Do you know who lies on this bed. Great people lie on this bed and spirits come to them as they sleep and spirits talk to them, communicate with them and program them and then in the morning they do the will of the spirits.
Evil, evil, evil, evil it has gone on for to long."

I see the bed catch on fire and burnt to ashes.

* * * * * * *

In Germany I see a palm tree rise out of the land and it is flexing its muscles. It is green and lush, healthy looking but it has no roots.

Saturday 7th July 2012.
Trinidad and Tobago. "I am about to judge this land with a flood and a shaking.

Wickedness is planted in this land and the hearts of man beat opposite to Me. Lies thrives and wickedness prevails. The Church will also be judged. The good, good, good ones."

Monday 9thth July 2012.
"Deception is in My House. Liars preach My word and deceivers profit."

Sunday 26th August 2012.
"Watchman of Uganda I call you."

I see a man in the atmosphere over Uganda and he is taking big chains from around his neck and casting them aside. He is also taking chains off of his ankle and wrist.

"A great work is coming for them, a greater season. O what a fire. Every corner of this land will know the work of the Lord. I will touch the depths of this land. The heaviness is removed but a season is coming where I will go deep and strong foundations for Me will be established.
Many times you will call Me and many times I will show you what I have for this land, the heartbeat of the continent."

Monday 3rd September 2012.
I saw a military plane in the sky then it dived underwater.

"They are developing a plane that would also operate underwater. Nothing is hidden from
Me. My eyes are on the earth. I search all things, I know all things, I permit and I destroy, I allow and I holdback. I AM GOD.
God of all the heavens and all the earth. All is Mine and they must know."

* * * * * * *

I see a pen travel down towards Brazil and touches it. It makes a dot on Brazil and the ink of it spreads out over the land in a circular fashion.

"One little touch from Me and I can saturate that whole nation. I am doing a work. They will rise, they will rise and others will be helped. I am changing their perspective, I am changing the people. How they see themselves will change. I am about to change many nations."

* * * * * * *

"Ecuador, the doors have began to open and nothing will close it, nothing shall stop My hand. I move you and I make you into who I want."

* * * * * * *

I see Russia lift out of its place and flips then lands upside down.

"Everything is about to be turned. Everything is about to be turned upside down. They have been warned son. They have been greatly warned. The pride of that man, the pride and boasting of that man. It's a stench to Me it's a stench. I will knock him off his horse and I will break the legs of his pride. He has no respect for Me son, absolutely no respect."

* * * * * * *

Lithuania, I see a jug pouring milk on the head of a baldhead man. He looked out of shape with a punch belly but as the milk is poured on his head he becomes healthy and muscular. He stands up and shouts "thank you Lord!"

"Milk first, I send the milk first."

* * * * * * *

Yugoslavia, I see the two mountains slam together and a lightening rod welds them so no separation.

"They are stubborn son and some don't want to bury old differences."

Friday 7th September 2012.
I see wild stallions being held back in a safe place.

"These are the young ministers I am holding back until the time. Nothing shall stop them and nothing shall stand in their way. No law, no constitution."

I see a stallion kicking with his back legs.

"They shall kick and break many things. Hard and dry things will be broken."

* * * * * * *

"I give the nations a very short time of peace, a very short time. But then I will pound the earth, and pound the earth, and pound the earth."

I see a fist pounding the earth.

Monday 10th September 2012.
"They have been warned. Many of them who do spiritual wickedness have been warned. My sword is about to pass through your land and I will have no favor. A dreadful time, a very dreadful time."

Monday 8th October 2012.

I see a hand holding a little strainer made of wire mesh. The United States is poured into the strainer. When I looked into the strainer I saw little rocks of gold but the gold became tarnished and black. Milk was then poured on the rocks and the tarnish left as the rocks returned to its original gold.

The hand then started moving the strainer up and down as the gold rocks bounced around in the strainer.

"Nothing will be the same again. Many things are going to be moved around. State after state will be touched. I bring permanent change."

Sunday 25th November 2012.

I see Mexico folded as a scroll with a red string tied around it as a bow.

"I have plans for them. It will be unfolded in times and in seasons as I will it. Greater things are coming to this place. Greater things are coming to this people. I have special plans."

I see a broom sweeping in Mexico.

"First I will do some cleaning and I will start with My house. You know I miss nothing, to the smallest detail, not a speck. You will see the beginning of great things in Mexico. I send a boom and I raise the economy. Even America will be helped. I am God and I turn things around. Now I command the scroll to unfold."

I see the scroll unfold and Mexico is looking like a heart, red in color and beating.

"I increase the life, I increase the flow, I increase the strength."

"Their will be a government for Me and the guns will be laid down, the narcotics will die."

* * * * * * *

"Cuba, rapid change, rapid, rapid changes. I waited and waited. Say goodbye to the old guard. I send a new day, new government. The deliverance of a people."

I see a black mist on the people but the breadth of God blows it away and the people rise from under the mist, strong and rejoicing.

* * * * * * *

"Venezuela, you have mesmerized the world with your beautiful women but I put My foot down and I take away your beauty."

Monday 10th December 2012.
Mark 7:1-3. Then the Pharisees and some of the scribes came together to Him, having come from Jerusalem. Now when they saw some of His disciples eat bread with defiled, that is, with unwashed hands, they found fault. For the Pharisees and all the Jews do not eat unless they wash their hands <u>in a special way, holding the tradition of the elders.</u> NKJV.

"Many times they hinder My body, son, many times they stop the progress. Those in leadership, high positions and lofty positions who love to crack the whip. Many of them are like an abscess, a boil to cause illness. So I turn it around and make their body sick as they did to My Church it now plagues them. Many I want to heal."

* * * * * * *

Tuesday 18th December 2012.
"I am not finished with Barack Obama. Son, he will bring peace. He will cause both ends to be welded, welded together. The black and the white. They are separated.

I see two rods. One on the right and one on the left. One white and one black. But then they bend or curve towards each other and as both tips touch each other a welding takes place and its difficult to look straight at it because of the glair.
The welded parts are red hot but in time they cool off and now the rod looks like one strong rod of iron as if it was never separated or welded.

"You have seen right and do not doubt, son. Do not doubt."

Thursday 20th December 2012.
Costa Rica, I see an envelope and as it is opened a post card comes out. On the out side it has red decorations but as it is opened the inside is empty. A hand with a pen writes in the post card, closes it, and returns it to the envelope and sends it down to Costa Rica.

"I send to them My promises and I never lie."

Sunday 23rd December 2012.
I see a brown dove fly out of Martinique and it travels towards the sky. The dove turns into an owl and the owl turns into an eagle.

* * * * * * *

Ipswich, I see a man with a shovel digging next to what looks like a creek or stream but he is getting tired.

"I will wear them out. Their plans will not come to pass."

Thursday 3rd January 2013.
"Ecuador, I close one door and I leave the others open. It has begun son, it has begun."

* * * * * * *

In Johannesburg I see a white clock tower, made of concrete with a pyramid shape at the top. The part of the tower with the clock breaks off and falls to the ground.

"His time is up, his time is up."

I see South Africa in the form of a book and a hand turns the page.

"South Africa I give you a new day, a new page. More chapters to be written."

I see a hand passing over South Africa from east to west and the hand is bringing a cloud or mist on the country.

"I will saturate them. My revival is coming, My visitation is coming."

* * * * * * *

Belize, I see two hands holding an open book with nothing written in it. A drawing of Belize appears in the book. It jumps out of the book and starts dancing.

"They will never forget Me, when I am finished doing what I have to, they will never forget Me."

* * * * * * *

"Ecuador, I will fashion you into all that I want you to be. The outside will not have a hold. I will fashion you."

* * * * * * *

"Jerusalem, Jerusalem, Jerusalem great things are coming."

* * * * * * *

I see a man wearing cowboy clothes and a skeleton wearing cowboy clothes. The two are facing each other as if it was a gunfight.

"America is still trying to solve problems with an old fashioned gunfight."

I see a great axe hit the ground between the two gunfighters and the earth shakes and splits. With the great shaking the skeleton falls to the ground and he breaks apart and the other man falls to the ground and then puts himself in a sitting position and he is looking at the great split in the ground that looks like a canyon, and he is in amazement.

Monday 7th January 2013.
"Trinidad and Tobago, floods are coming, floods are coming, floods are coming."

Monday 14th January 2013.
"Warnings, warning, warning I send to Nigeria. I will split you in two if you do not repent I will split you."

* * * * * * *

"Justice will prevail in the United Nations. My people I am raising up, My people I will put in place, My people will take the helm. My people rise! My people rise! No more mimicking around."

I see a mouse in a room and it is running from corner to corner.

"Stop this says God. Find your place and do not be moved."

* * * * * * *

"I shall torch the nations. A fire is coming where the heat will be unbearable. Many will cry out and many will be consumed. But the stubborn will be consumed. I will make some dry and their land will be dry. A famine here and a famine their. Famine in the most unlikely places. Not a drop of water and the earth will cry out and tremble. I will cause the earth to rage in anger, I will cause the earth to refuse. The more they sacrifice to their gods, the more they give to their gods, the more I take away."

I see a torch above the earth and it tilts towards the earth and the whole earth is ablaze.

January 2013
"Bahamas. Mene, Mene, Tekel, Upharsin."

Thursday 17th January 2013.
"Swift action I take, swift action I take, son. Many governments on the earth think they are brighter than I am. Many governments on the earth are not for the people. Many governments on the earth are for their own gain so swift action I take. A fall here, and an exposure over there. Some shaken and some will have the place where they are standing removed from under them. But I will be swift and I have no favorites. I do rule."

Friday 18th January 2013.
January prayer and fast. "I don't respect it. Tell them I don't respect it. Many of them cannot wait for January to finish for lust and gluttony to rule again. And many of them lie. Let them know I look at motive. That is what I look at."

Saturday 19th January 2013.
"West Indies, be warned. If you miss the call the favor will shift to the East Indies."

* * * * * * *

"Watchman of Germany, I call you."

I see a man in the clouds above Germany. He is strong and muscular. He has a bald head with beard and mustache, no shirt on him and he is dressed as a boxer with gloves, pants and shoes. He is standing in a fighting position.

"Many boxing matches are coming but I will give Germany the victory."

Thursday 14th February 2013.
"The future leaders of the Church will not be bible school students and they will be like wild stallions."

Sunday 24th March 2013.
I see a cauldron in the atmosphere over Trinidad. In the cauldron are a variety of colored ribbons.

"They are trying many things and trying a mixture to get a solution but no solution will come. I will expose them son, I will expose their hidden things. Oh, if I were to show you their hidden and covered things. The lies, I turn My face because of the lies and some of them behave as if they are god. I will humiliate them, I will greatly humiliate them.
Those who say they know Me have compromised and they know the lies and pretend. I turn My back to them.
Trouble is on its way. I will cause the laws on the outside to deal with the man who is rooted in corruption. They will take him away. I have had enough of him and his whole family is rotten to the core."

Monday 1st April 2013.
"You are about to find out who they are. They will expose themselves. They will dig and dig to find anything to use."

Wednesday 30th October 2013.
"They are like rats searching for anything they can find. They are like rats digging in your past. They are like rats, any garbage makes them

feel good about them self and what they are doing. They have caused many to turn from Me. "Mark those who cause division." They will use it, they will continually use it."

Monday 25th November 2013.
Ministers and others who leave their body and come to my home. " They come to your house to look for evidence but I know their hearts, I know what is hidden inside of them."

Monday 6th January 2014.
"Money for honey, money for honey. That is what is in My house. Prostitution! I keep telling you prostitution is in My house and the leaders are feeding it. They brought it in.
This is My word and you will fear no man and you will deliver it."

If you have read this book of prophecy you now have more than enough proof that Jesus the Christ is real, He is all that He says He is and He rules.

You may think you have ruler ship but there is a Ruler above you.

You now know that He is the Judge but He can also bless, maintain and sustain. He also rules all nations big and small and no nation or government is mightier than He is.
You now have decisions to make. You can choose Jesus or you can reject Him and face the consequences. If you choose Jesus you have made the wisest and safest decision any human being can make

Romans 10: 9-10. That if you confess with your mouth the Lord Jesus and believe in your heart that God has raised Him from the dead, you will be saved. For with the heart one believes unto righteousness, and with the mouth confession is made unto salvation. Nkjv.

Prayer of Salvation

Please pray this prayer from the honest intent of your heart.

* * * * * * * * *

Lord Jesus, I acknowledge You as King and Ruler of all the earth and I now ask You to be King and Ruler of my life. I have sinned and I repent asking You to forgive me of all my sins, come into my life and make me the kind of person You want me to be. Holy Spirit, come into my life and be my best friend as you daily talk to me and guide me. Jesus the Christ is now my Lord and Savior, I am saved. Amen.

* * * * * * * * *

Direction for new members of the family

Please find a true Church that will give you the truth about God and the full gospel of His Son Jesus the Christ. They will take you to baptism and your life will be transformed.

Do not look back and do not step back but walk with Jesus and build a growing relationship with Him.

The first year with Jesus

The ingredients for this relationship is: prayer, read and believe the bible, daily interaction with the Holy Spirit and fellowship with other Christians who belong to the Body of Christ.

Jesus loves you and He will never leave you.

Prayer for your nation

Repent on the behalf of your nation for the sins that have been committed. What Jesus is looking at is the honest intent of your heart and not a religious formality.

* * * * * * * * *

Lord Jesus, King and Ruler of all the earth. I repent of my sins and the sins of my nation. We have sinned against You and All Mighty God and I know that your judgment is true but I ask forgiveness for all of us.

Forgive us of past and present sins. Those that are known and those that were done in secret because I know You see and know all things and nothing is hidden from Your eyes.

I ask for Your mercy and grace to be upon us. As a people we have gone the wrong way but there is still time to turn to You.

I repent on the behalf of those who have founded our nation and the sins they have committed, I repent on the behalf of past and present leaders and the sins they have committed.

Have Your way with my nation, have Your way with the present and the future of my nation. Help us to submit to You and have

Your way Lord Jesus.

I hand my nation over to the Lordship of Jesus the Christ. And we repent.

* * * * * * * * * *

PRAYER FOR THE CHURCH.

We repent on the behalf of the Church fathers and mothers who established teachings that seemed right but it was wrong, open our eyes Lord.

We repent on the behalf of Church fathers and mothers who gave us doctrines and structures with Your word but You never ordained it, open our eyes Lord.

We repent on the behalf of present day Church fathers and mothers who don't want to let go of old dead things that is only a hindrance to Your body and the things they have brought in that is not of

You, open our eyes Lord and use us to throw those things out.

We repent on the behalf of our brothers and sisters who only know you on Sunday morning, give them a great hunger for You lord.

Lord Jesus return to Your house and take back Your place. Come quickly Lord Jesus.

We pray for a cleaning out of the five fold ministry. Lord Jesus, there are lodge men and lodge women holding positions in Your house. Bring them to repentance from the heart and if they don't then do what must be done.

There are warlocks and witches in Your house. Bring them to repentance from the heart and if they don't then do what must be done.

It is Your house Lord Jesus so touch what others don't want to touch and do a cleaning work. The spirits of the lodge is rebuked and driven out of the pulpit, out of the church departments and out of the pews.

We command religious spirits, witchcraft, theological and doctrinal minds who only see things one way and those who are using the Church for their own gain to get out and they are permanently blocked from returning.

We declare the will of Jesus be done in every part of the Body of Christ with a radical, none compromising and fearless Spirit with no favoritism.

Do it Lord Jesus and our faith says it is done and nothing will change it.

Come and take back Your Church Lord Jesus, come quickly.

Glory to God.

The Fray

THE

FRAY.

HELL IN THE HOLY HOUSE.

A REPORT BY ANTHONY WHARTON.

SUNDAY 10TH APRIL 2016.

A fray is a series of events to destroy your life or ministry or bring you under the control of other people. They use witchcraft, technological devices and what ever issues they can find out about you. They will watch you in the spirit and in the natural and study you to make up their plans. They will use channeling on you to find out past events that are even in your childhood. Channeling can be used to find out your plans for your life, your business and other peoples business so confidentiality can be broken.

They use witchcraft for others to believe you are loosing your mind.

They can use technology to superimpose on your home, workplace or school.

One of their tricks is to deceive people by telling them they are helping you with some of your problems. But they don't tell people everything they are doing.

Oxford Dictionary: Affect with fear, frighten, be afraid, tremble, shudder with fear, make a disturbance, assault, attack and drive off, frighten or scare away.

WITCHES HATE YOUR INTIMACY WITH THE HOLY SPIRIT SO THEY WILL DO WHAT EVER IT TAKES TO GET YOU TO GRIEVE OR QUENCH THE HOLY SPIRIT.

Christian witches will try to get you out of the will of God so you will obey the will and plans they have for you.

THIS IS WHAT GOD SAID.

A word from years ago: " The craft has root in My Church and it has been allowed and I will show you greater than you already know."

This is what God said about the Fray, Hook and Drag.
" I hate it, I hate it. It is sick and weak."

God said three spirits are using them. Lust is the general demon that is feeding and pushing the fray.
1. Fear.
2. Jealousy.
3. Racism.

Sunday 3rd April 2016.
" Its not about Me it have nothing to do with Me. What they are doing to you are of their own will to bring darkness into your life. They are empty looking to be filled with someone else's wealth. They want your gold, they want your diamonds, they want the rich things I have put inside of you (They come in the spirit of my home and write down and record the revelations, prophecies and songs that I receive from God). You are not

the only one they are sourcing, you are not the only one they are plugging into. You have seen them in your house, you have seen them writing your stuff, do not be afraid,
I told you their system is failed, they are using a failed system. It failed before they started it on you. No progress they have not progressed.
They want to know what is in your mind, they want to know the wealth of your mind (this is why they source my mind). Jealousy have brought them against your eyes. They want to dim your eyes, son. They want to dim your eyes. They want to connect to your spirit. Everything you know, they must know. Everything you hear, they must hear. Their family line is not so spotless so they dig for spots in your family line. The pirating is true, son. And the raping of spirit is true. They are not afraid to take your wealth. It have nothing to do with sin in your life they gave themselves an assignment that have already failed. They count your money for you to believe you need their help, they want it to look like you need their help. Their mouth have no covering, son. Their mouth have no covering. They thought you wanted something from them, they thought they were going to be overthrown. You have chosen My way, son. You have chosen My road. Their minds are not where it is supposed to be.
They say your mind is not right and they have told it to others for you to be reduced. They are about defending themselves it have nothing to do with Me. All their technology have failed because I AM GREATER.
They have abused you, in the spirit they have abused you but what is coming to them is sure. The little boys got a toy to play with, the little boys got an assignment I never gave them. I told you, you will always be ahead of them and you know why? Because it is My will.
They have scorned your name, they have tried to put scorn on your name but I wash and I wash.
They keep track of you because of fear, they want to know everything you do and everywhere you go. Their fear tried to get you frightened but you have been bold."

I see the idol they speak through.

" That is the idol they use it gives them nothing but an empty view. They want to turn your mind into darkness but your visions will be greater. They want to create an environment around you where no one trust you. They want to create an environment where no one sees you as a true minister. You owe them nothing, son you owe them nothing and the anointing is strong and this is My voice. Their tricks remember their tricks.
They behave as if they own you. They behave as if you are their property in your own house but watch as I do a quick work and their departure is to be recognized and others will tell you. They come in the spirit, they come in their spirit but not in My spirit. They want you to do their bidding. They want you to believe they have authority over you but you have submitted to My authority. They try to create traffic in your spirit so you wont hear Me clearly but I speak oh so loudly."

Tuesday 5th April 2016.
" Your enemies are dead walking in the land of the living. They come at the early times to torment you but see deeper and see their dark ways and their hidden devils as they

torment themselves with their own spirit of hate. Look and see clearly, son. Look and see clearly. Their hate is internal coming out at you. It is on their inside tormenting them. They cannot have what you have and it torments them."

These are some of the words that was used to try and break me when they came in the spirit.

" I don't care, you are not mad but I will send you mad."
" I am your maker."
" You have to stay in Trinidad and serve your black people."
" You don't like your own people."
" No body want you."
" We will bring down your ministry."
" You have to come down from that high place."
" You have to come back to our church and beg for forgiveness."
" We will drain the anointing out of you."
" You owe us."
" We will take away your spiritual eyes."
" I don't care, you cannot be more powerful then me."
" We will tell them you have issues so you cannot go anywhere."

They boast in what they do and can even use deception to make it look as if they are trying to help you by taking charge of your life.

They always talk to me in the spirit and do things for me to react like a madman.

They are always at my home.

In the spirit they put a scope on your eyes to block your spiritual sight and show you what they want you to see.

They try to source your mind for ideas or your business. They also source your spirit.

In the spirit they also use microphones, cameras, speakers and projectors.

They superimpose and use witchcraft to get close to you. Your home, school, workplace etc.

<u>They use deception for others to believe you are loosing your mind.</u>

I saw a dark room made with black curtains and in the room was a mirror. It looked like an office area.

5. I don't understand everything, but the camera can send the images of the human mind to deceive the mind and eyes.

TV screen with images

6. This can be a mannequin or emblem representing the person. They put spirit on it. I call it the voodoo doll effect.

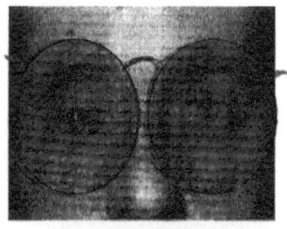

The scope or a glass with a camera on it is used to send images to the mind and deceive the eyes. This is also used to take pictures or record everything you see. This can also damage your spiritual or physical eyes. It is used to take pictures of private information.

This Virtual Reality Headset is placed on a mannequin representing the person they are doing evil to. Because the mannequin has a spirit on it the person sees everything they send to the headset so they can feed the individual false images and visions, but the Holy Spirit will bring truth and true visions.

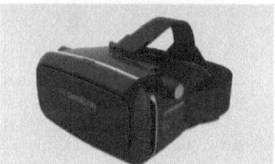

7. In the spirit, this is placed on your head to source your mind for ideas, your vision for life, people's business, or to send messages to your mind to control you. This includes pictures. This can be used to put you to sleep or wake you from sleep. Your ideas can also be sourced or channeled by the mind of a witch plugging into yours.

They can also come in the spirit and put their hand on your head to impart, extract, or put you to sleep.

135

8. This can be a form of spiritually raping the person.

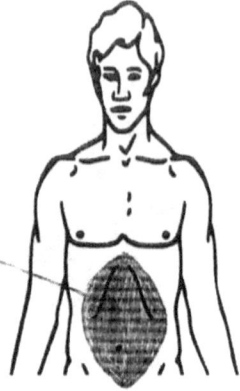

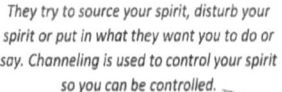
They try to source your spirit, disturb your spirit or put in what they want you to do or say. Channeling is used to control your spirit so you can be controlled.

Your prayer life can be controlled.

9. They come in the spirit with projectors to project images so you can be deceived.

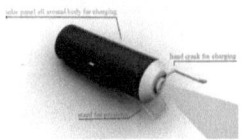 

Witches use black cloth or black backgrounds, to project images to deceive and manipulate those who see it. They are in the spirit and try to deceive you when you are in the physical, so they can give you false visions.

10. A person with a speaker on them <u>will come in the spirit to harass you</u> with noise. It is meant to cause disturbance. He can also have a camera. This can also be used for various people to speak to you. <u>They can also use voices of people you know</u> so you can attack them.

11. They use technology to superimpose on your home, school, work place, etc. They can be in your home and you don't know it. This can be used with astral travelling.

12. I call this Shadowing. The spirit of one or more than one person come on you. This is to harass, intimidate or break you down. It can be used to pull anointing or energy from you and also source or influence the mind. They want to see what you see and know what you know which includes what you think about. You can feel the pain or injuries of the person shadowing you. At times they will reveal themselves for others to believe you are also involved in witchcraft. When witchcraft cannot defeat you they will try to make it look like you are also a witch.

13. I saw something shaped like this. This can also have the voodoo doll effect. They put spirit on it and it represents your body. They can put a microphone in it and they hear and record everything in your spirit. It can also be reversed and they will put what they want in your spirt or speak to you. They can also put a speaker in it. They can cause pain and do other things to your body just as the voodoo doll effect. This can be used to get your ideas, vision or goals, messages for ministry and revelations etc. this can also be <u>used to source</u> your energy or anointing.

This have spirits in it. The black hole has speakers, microphones, or even smells. They can extract bad information and use it.

14. They superimpose on your vehicle and watch you in the spirit. This can be used to harass you, cause accidents or cause mechanical or electrical problems in your vehicle. They can astral travel with this.

15. They superimpose on your house or workplace. This can be used to mind your business, harass you or collect evidence against you. Astral travel can also be sued with this.

   N.B.: Superimpose is when technology is used with spirit, cameras and light to transfer an object from one place to put it on or near another object. GPS may be used.

16. This is sourcing and also channeling. They will see your thoughts or ideas on a computer or television screen. They can also go into your memory and take out pictures or ideas. They can also put ideas or images in your mind. This can be used to steal messages or revelations from ministers. They will use this to try and block visions from God.

The TV or computer can be at different locations from the person being sourced, but superimposing or channeling can connect.

17. This can be channeling to source ideas or send messages to your brain. This can also be used with one-person spirit sourcing another person spirit to find out your goals, visions, ideas, preaching, messages, revelations or whatever is in your spirit.

Each person can be at separate locations.

18. When you are sleeping or resting they can spiritually enter your home and source the spirit of your mind or your human spirit. This is to try and to get the anointing, source things from your life and your past, goals, vision, dreams, etc. these people can enter your home in the spirit to steal your ideas, vision, preaching messages etc. while you are sleeping they will also try to program your mind and spirit with the messages they want. They especially love the things of your past and they feast on any nasty thing.

19. They use technology with a spirt of witchcraft to hook up the person so they can reduce or increase their energy levels. You can feel tired or sleepy even if you have rested and in good health. The craft is based on controlling lives so they will use many forms to do it.

Witches use this pole to keep your spirit so they can manipulate and try to control. It is a pole specifically used to do their witchcraft and it can locate the person's spirit anytime they want to.

20. Witches use the lower left side that is just above the hip bone to use it as an entry point to your spirit. They can put spirit on a mannequin or something that represents you and in your lower left side you will feel what they are doing. This can be used to get what they want from you or put in things to harm you. A witch can put their finger or hand on that area and channel to your spirit what he wants your spirit to receive so he can get you to say what he wants or he want you to do. You can feel pain in that area which means they are interfering with you.

They will interfere with your navel to cause disturbance to your spirit and this can also cause health problems. You can feel pain in your navel area and this means the craft is interfering with you.

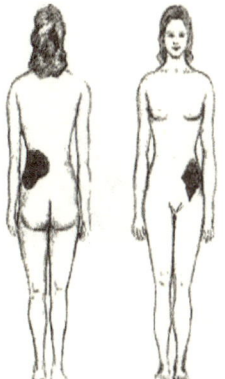

21. Witch can send or channel from their brain to the brain of a person or persons. This is mind control which can give false visions and dreams, witchcraft ideas which oppose Christ ideas, it comes against the mind of Christ and the spirit of the mind, the witch can know all your thoughts and your visions. This can also cause pain. This can be used to source your ideas or vision.

A witch can send or channel messages to unsuspecting Christians for a number of reasons. To control the person or persons, to send false messages deceiving them into thinking they heard from God. To use them to turn against someone, to get them on the side of the witch, to get the majority vote in decision making or to turn them against the person who is telling the truth. A witch can also extract information from your spirit which is spiritually raping you. Witches can use a computer instead of a witch. You can be electronically hooked up in the spirit while they rape your mind and spirit.

22. I call this scavenger bird or corbeaux mind. They are always digging into your life for your past situations that Jesus have released you from. They love to feast on the filthy dead things and bring it to the surface and give life to it.

They will use the craft and a computer to store information. They will dig and dig to the pit of your spirit and scrape the bottom of it to find old dead garbage that God have forgiven, you have forgiven and moved on and some things you cannot remember. This is the craft at work and the deceived will use deception on you so their stuff can come to the surface and they are deceived into thinking it is your garbage. A deliverance minister who is moved **"By the Spirit of God"** will find things that God want to deal with but the scavenger or corbeaux will dig for stuff by another spirit.

23. This is a mannequin or anything that represents the person they are working on. They put spirit on it. When they do things to it they person can feel it and they can also hook it up electronically.

    They can use various emblems to represent body parts and this can also have a voodoo doll effect.

24. They come in the spirit to put handcuffs on the person to keep them bound or arrested spiritually

25. They can use rope or anything to bind you in the spirit. They come in the spirit to bind your feet, to hinder your progress or keep you where they want you.

26. This is a sketch or a picture of the person they are working on.
They speak curses and make witchcraft declarations on it.

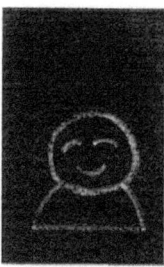

27. I saw a scaffolding with a representation of a vehicle on top. This is used to have access to the person they are working on. They can use other emblems, depending on where the person is, driving etc.

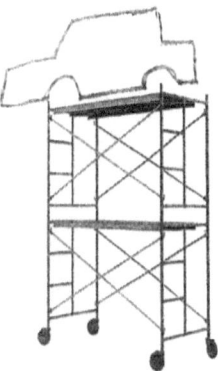

28. These people can stand on the pulpit and preach to you or sit next to you in the pews and feel no remorse or conviction.

29. **Lust is Feeding**

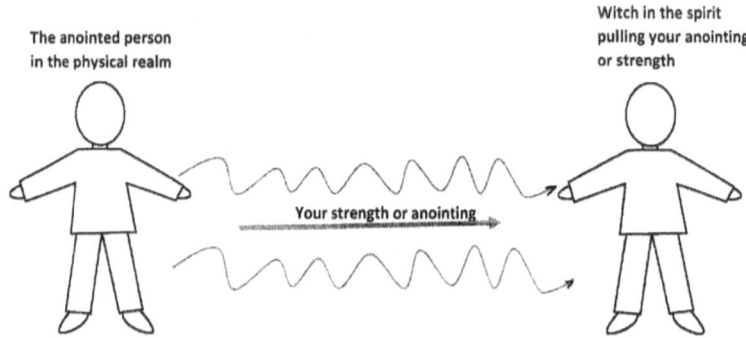

In the spirit it will look like a wave coming off of the anointed person. The witch is pulling it off the anointed person to enhance the craft. Lust is one of the major demons that drives and feeds the craft. Witches will always want what you have and they are never satisfied. You can feel sudden tiredness or a drop in the anointing.

30.

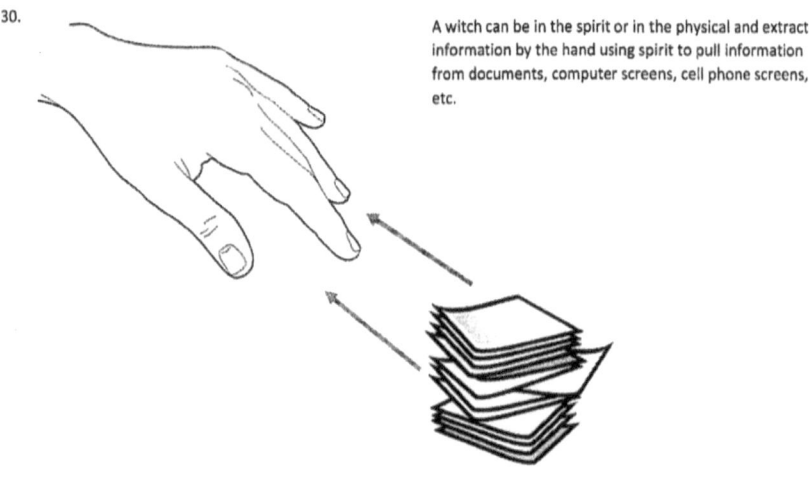

A witch can be in the spirit or in the physical and extract information by the hand using spirit to pull information from documents, computer screens, cell phone screens, etc.

I have shown you some of the works of the craft that witches who pretend to be Christian are using. Be sharp, be aware and be non-compromising because they are full of tricks.

31.

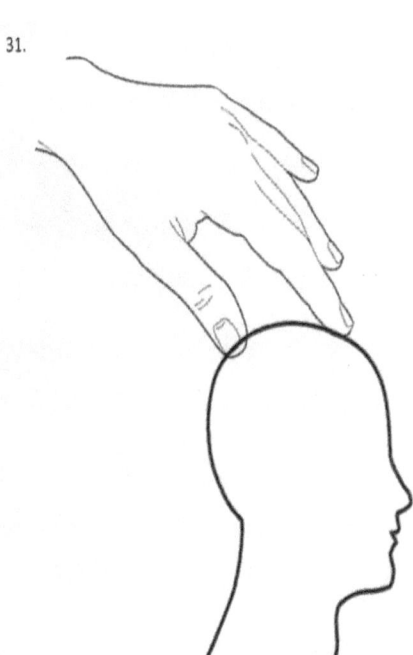

You can be awake but it is mostly when you are asleep witches can lay hands on your head or spirit man and impart what they want or extract information; such as, your business, other people's business, ideas, visions, dreams, goals, and they can also dig up things from your past.

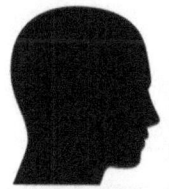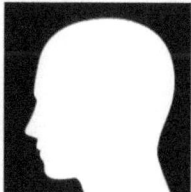

A witch can come in the spirit while you are in the physical watching television, driving, or any fixed position, and they can lock into your eyes, which is the window to your soul. This can be used to transfer demons, contaminate your mind, get you to think how they want. This can also be used to drain/pull energy or strength from you mind. You can feel a burning in your eyes or some heaviness on your face.

32.'

The witch is in the spirit and speaking sleep and slumber over the life of the individual. This gives the witch a feeling of power over you and boasting rights, but know that a witch has deep self-hate, rejection and feels unfulfilled. Sometimes you can hear the witch in the spirit speaking those words. This method can be used to cast spells or even put lust on you. If you fall to sin, the witch who is pretending to be a minister will use the evidence, but know who you are in Christ, and know that you belong to Him.

33. Witches come in the spirit with various instruments to harass you. Some of them are pronging fork, sticks, buzzers, high-wattage light to burn you, heat packs, etc.

Witches attack seven (7) points of the body:
1. The base of the spine
2. Spleen
3. Navel
4. Heart
5. Throat
6. Between the eyes
7. The top of the head

Witches will also interfere with your private parts.

Witches can also orchestrate the destroying of your relationships and orchestrate the relationship they want you in.

Tuesday 24th May, 2016

"We already have things in place for when your report comes out, we have people to say it is madness, he is mad."

"Nobody in Trinidad will believe we are doing those things; we will say you are mad."

I am Anthony Wharton, called by Jesus to be a Prophet like Ezekiel and a governing Apostle of Apostle of governance. I belong to Jesus, the Christ.

REMEMBER TO GET MY FIRST BOOK.

GOD
THE SUPREME EXAMPLE OF MAN

By
Anthony Wharton

Available at WestBow Press.

- Knowing your true identity.
- Money answers all things.
- Jesus was never poor.
- Mobilized financial strength.
- Wealth that cannot be seen.
- Marriage and the mighty covenant keepers.
- The sexy idol.
- The broken woman and the healed woman.
- The woman, the being for an important function.
- Competition in the body.
- The mother of all living.
- Escaping satan's assignment.
- The MAD men.
- The man and his Masters Degrees.
- Nation builders.
- The man and the woman, one ministry.
- And much, much more in my first book.

Anthony Wharton Contacts

Anthony Wharton

1 (868) 770-9964.

Facebook

Twitter

www.ingramcontent.com/pod-product-compliance
Lightning Source LLC
Chambersburg PA
CBHW030117100526
44591CB00009B/429